Wealth's Wake-Up Call: Rethinking Riches and Eternity

By

William Amofah

Copyright © 2024
All Rights Reserved

Contents

Preface *4*
Greed is good *12*
Accounting for Greed *36*
Doing God's Work *60*
Happy Money *90*
A Salary of Smoke *106*
The Cost of Living: A Monetary Phenomenon *125*
"We are the 99 Percent" *140*
The Gospel of Wealth *160*
Greatest Opportunity Cost *179*
Acknowledgements *194*

Preface

IF YOU WERE a young man in the bloom of life, handsome, of robust physique, cultured, possessed five million dollars, unmarried, what would you do? That was the question The Chicago Tribune posed to its readers in the fall of 1921 following a young millionaire's decision to become a missionary to China. So stunned by the decision, the paper splashed the news story across its front pages with the headline, 'YOUNG MILLIONAIRE RENOUNCES WORLD TO BE MISSIONARY.' [1] The subject of the piece was William Whiting Borden. Born on November 1, 1887, in Cook County, Chicago, Illinois, he was the son of William and Mary De Garmo Borden.

Along with his three siblings, John, Mary, and Joyce, he was set to inherit the Borden family fortune, which had been made through silver mining operations in Colorado. A

---

[1] https://vancechristie.com/tag/william-borden/

partner of Marshall Field, Bill's father was a mining engineer and an adventurer and, in his lifetime, led expeditions in the Bering Sea north of the Arctic Circle. However, it was his mother's conversion to Christianity in 1984 that changed the course of his future. Devoted to his mother, William would often attend church service with his mum on Sunday mornings at Chicago Avenue Church (now known as the Moody Tabernacle), which was pastored by R.A. Torrey, a well-known American evangelist and teacher. It was there that William, at the age of seven, had his first communion and dedicated his life to Christ, thus becoming a full-time member of the church. He attended University School and Latin and Manual Training School before going to 'The Hill,' a high school in Pottstown, Pennsylvania, at 14, where he graduated at the top of his class. For his high school graduation present, William and Mary gave 16-year-old Borden a trip around the world. However, as the young man travelled through Asia, the Middle East, and Europe[2], he felt a growing burden for the world's hurting people, writing to his parents, "I have so much of everything in this life, and there are so many millions who have nothing and live in

---

[2] https://www2.cbn.com/article/integrity/no-regrets-william-bordens-inspiring-leadership

darkness! I don't think it is possible to realize it until one sees the East. I know that it is no easy thing to serve the Lord, but others have been enabled to do so, and there is no reason why I should not. Mark 10.27." This is when he set his sights on becoming a missionary. (It was claimed that one of his friends expressed disbelief that Bill was "throwing himself away as a missionary.")

Upon returning home from his gap year, William entered Yale, where he immediately jumped into his studies and the various social activities the university had to offer. One of them was a bible study group. "Our prayer group started with just us two, but by the end of our sophomore year, it had grown so large that it had to be divided. Similar groups were meeting in each of the classes. [3] This movement began with the first-year students and moved up to the seniors rather than vice versa. And the Lord really answered our prayers— a number of men were converted," said Charlie Campbell, a friend of Borden. Purposed initially as a college for training men to minister the gospel, Yale was founded in 1701 and has always had deeply religious roots and has been marked by various spiritual revivals in the past – only this time, it

---

[3] https://today.bju.edu/president/borden-yale-revival/

was more prominent as almost 1,000 out of the total of 1,300 Yale students ended up attending these Bible studies.

After graduating from Yale, and despite receiving many lucrative offers from Wall Street, William went to Princeton Seminary, where he prepared for a life of ministry. He spent two years at Theology college before planning a one-way trip to Egypt, where he wanted to learn Arabic to reach Muslims with the gospel despite his father writing him a letter at the time – that he would never have a job in the family business.

Nevertheless, William arrived in Cairo eagerly and set to work at once. But within a week, he was struck down with spinal meningitis. He took the prescribed treatments - but to no avail. Within a month, William Borden was dead. He died at the tender age of 25.[4] There was an outpouring of grief not just among friends and family but also across the world. A talented and passionate graduate was struck down in the prime of his life seeking to do God's will. To many, it seemed like such a waste. But that was not William's perspective. In the days before he died, he wrote, "No regrets." These two

---

[4] https://www.christianitytoday.com/history/2017/february/forgotten-final-resting-place-of-william-borden.html

words sum up the generous, no going back heart of William Borden. William took advantage of every way he had been made rich so that he'd be generous at every opportunity. He didn't live a long life. But a full life. A life full of love for God and others. He was a rich man who could squeeze through the eye of a needle.

****

The inspirational story of William Borden runs counter to today's culture, where there is a desperation for money, fame, and success. But the question is, why do we care so much about chasing that extra dollar? I mean, can it really bring us THAT much happiness? Indeed, while writing his autobiography, American businessman and philanthropist Michael Bloomberg came to the stark conclusion that "The reality of great wealth is that you can't spend it and you can't take it with you." [5]Furthermore, when John D. Rockefeller's accountant asked how much the multi-millionaire left when he died (he was the wealthiest man in the world in the 1930s), he was quoted as saying that his client "left it all, every last dime, taking nothing with him." This quote may seem obvious, but the truth is that we all come to the end of

---

[5] https://givingpledge.org/pledger?pledgerId=172

our lives as naked and empty-handed as on the day we were born. We can't take our riches with us. And yet, since the beginning of time, pursuing riches has been one of humanity's most significant priorities – sometimes at any cost. Some have even devoted their lives to amassing and retaining vast sums of money. But what profit is it to us if we gain the whole world but forfeit our soul? In other words, by focusing so much on wealth accumulation, we lose sight of our morality and the eternal destiny of our soul – which we cannot buy.

There's a great story in the New Testament Bible in which a wealthy young man, who was morally upright, was challenged to give up what he valued the most - his money - to follow Jesus; he was devastated because the price was too high. He wasn't willing to part with the "security" and luxury of cash. The Bible says he walked away "sorrowful" because he had "great riches." As a result, Jesus observed that it was "easier for a camel to go through the eye of a needle than for a rich man to get into heaven."

Some have taken this out of context and thought it meant that Warren Buffet, Bill Gates, and Mark Zuckerberg wouldn't make it to heaven, which is not entirely true. He was trying to say that no one can serve two masters – God and money, for either he will hate the one and love the other, or he will be devoted to the one and despise the other. In other words, we cannot serve both. Moreover, history has shown us that wealth can disappear in the blink of an eye (the Bible puts it more bluntly – saying that money "will sprout wings and fly away like an eagle.") One only has to look at the impact of COVID-19, the 2008 U.S. financial crisis, and the global recession that followed, where trillions of dollars were wiped off all the significant stock markets across the globe, jobs were lost, and many businesses went bust.

For that reason, in an age where more wealth isn't making people any happier, *Wealth's Wake-Up Call* attempts to expose the temporary nature of earthly wealth and urges the rich of this present age not to pin their hopes on the uncertainty of riches – which is here today and gone tomorrow - but to put their hope in the eternal God, who not only richly provides us with everything we could ever need. But who also promises that he'll never leave or forsake us – something that money can't promise. Therefore, God is the only safe investment for eternity.

"The point is that you can't be too greedy."

- President Donald Trump.

Greed is good

IN ARGUABLY ONE of the most memorable scenes in Olivier Stone's 1987 *Wall Street*, Gordon Gekko takes to the stage during an Annual General Meeting (AGM) to deliver a pitch to shareholders of the fictional company Teldar Paper:

"Well, ladies and gentlemen, we're not here to indulge in fantasy but in political and economic reality. America has become a second-rate power. Its trade deficit and its fiscal deficit are at nightmare proportions. Now, in the days of the free market, when our country was a top industrial power, there was accountability to the stockholder. The Carnegies, the Mellons, the men that built this great industrial empire, made sure of it because it was their money at stake. Today, management has no stake in the company!

The point is, ladies and gentlemen, is that Greed – for lack of a better word – is good. Greed is right. Greed works. Greed clarifies, cuts through, and captures the essence of the evolutionary spirit. Greed, in all of its forms – Greed for life, money, love, and knowledge – has marked the upward surge of mankind. And Greed – you mark my words – will not only save Teldar Paper but that other malfunctioning corporation called the USA...Thank you."

Released just two months after the stock market crash in October 1987, Oliver Stone's classic perfectly portrays the greed and excess on Wall Street during the late 1980s. Previously a pinstripe industry decorated with graduates from Ivy League schools such as Yale and Harvard, the nation's financial centre underwent a swift change where, in a blink of an eye, analysts and traders were being hired – not for their knowledge of economics, but for their street smarts. It was more about having a "feel" of the market than having a formal education. The young and ambitious knew they could make it big on the Street and live the flamboyant lifestyles they had always dreamed of and seen on the television if they worked long and punishing hours. Banking houses soon became awash with employees with slick black hair, wearing suspenders [braces], buying and selling gold and foreign currency in the early hours of the morning on the booming exchanges of Asia and Europe. Together with the latest advancements in technology, this new breed of Wall Streeter changed the culture of high finance. An industry that was once defined by its stability, values, and relationships has become obsessed with making short-term profits – sometimes even breaking the law to do so. This new mindset was partly encouraged by U.S. President Ronald Regan, who believed that his predecessors had crimped free markets by burdening them with too many government taxes, too much government spending, and too many regulations. In a campaign-style trip to the trading floor of the New York Stock Exchange during the mid-1980s, he declared that if legislators embraced tax overhauls, the US economy "will be free to expand to its full potential, driving the bears back into permanent hibernation. That's our economic program for the next four years; we're going to turn the bull loose." [6]His speech had the desired effect as markets were let loose as individuals who had never before bought stocks or bonds dabbled in investing, even if that meant putting money in a mutual fund or participating in their company 401(k) plans. The stock market soared as a result – generating billions of dollars – especially in the corporate takeover world, fuelled by the availability of cheap debt. Wall Street firms were expanding their workforces yearly

---

[6] https://www.latimes.com/archives/la-xpm-1985-03-28-mn-29064-story.html

and throwing money at anything that moved. Those who got pulled into that whirlwind found they could do no wrong. This led to increased profits and exposure for its top dealers, who soon made the front pages of TIME and Fortune magazine. The push for more money and bigger deals contributed to the public perception that capitalism had gone wild.

One of the kingpins of this fast-money era was Ivan Frederick Boesky. Born March 6, 1937, in Detroit, Michigan, Boesky was the son of Jewish Russian immigrants. His father, a restaurateur, owned chains of bars and restaurants in downtown Detroit. This entrepreneurial spirit soon rubbed off on his son, who drove an ice cream truck around the city at the age of Thirteen to make money - regularly staying out until Ten or Eleven at night. This often landed him in hot water with the cops because he went beyond his limited driving permit. [7]"The police were always stopping Ivan," recalled childhood friend David Fishman in an interview with *Vanity Fair*. "They would pick him up all the time and take him in, and his dad would have to go bail him out. That ice cream truck was a real pain in the neck to

---

[7] https://www.britannica.com/biography/Ivan-Boesky

his parents."[8] Although he attended several colleges, including Wayne State University, East Michigan University, and the University of Michigan, he failed to graduate with a Diploma. Nevertheless, he was admitted to the Detroit College of Law, graduating with a law degree in 1964. During this period, he met and married Seema Silberstein – daughter of the wealthy Detroit real estate developer Ben Silberstein, who owned the Beverly Hills Hotel in California. After relocating to New York in 1966, Boesky landed a job at the Wall Street Investment firm L.F. Rothschild Co. as a securities analyst. A year later, he moved on to First Manhattan. After a string of similar roles at several other brokerage firms, Boesky started his firm in 1975 following a $700,000 investment from his wife's family. His investment firm, which he called Ivan F. Boesky & Company L.P., was one of the first devoted solely to arbitrage.

In its simplest form, arbitrage involves purchasing a product, which is then immediately sold to make a profit. These transactions happen every day in the stock market and are a means to earn a profit from goods being sold at differing

---

[8] https://www.vanityfair.com/news/1993/01/ivan-boesky-199301

prices in varying markets. Boesky's business plan was to buy stocks in companies that appeared to be likely takeover targets. In such instances, the company's stock price that is taken over receives a big bounce, generating enormous profits for the firm or "arbitrageur" that had previously brought the company's stock at a far lower price. Takeover arbitrage was previously limited to a small group of old-line investment banks that invested in corporate mergers using their funds. Boesky, however, redefined the business by amassing stock on a scale never seen before and, often, sniffing out potential takeover targets rather than waiting for a deal to be announced. He was the first to raise vast pools of public money successfully and, in doing so, actually determined the fate of takeover battles. Over time, Boesky's company became very successful – outpacing the field by finding an "edge" in the market. One industry insider conceded to *The New York Times*, "He's the best in the business…He's made more money than any of us, making him the best." [9]By 1983, *Forbes Magazine* listed Boesky as one of the wealthiest 400 Americans – estimating his net worth to be around $150 million. Despite his eccentric

---

[9] https://www.nytimes.com/1984/06/24/business/top-arbitrager-ivan-f-boesky-the-secretive-life-of-an-arb.html

personality, he was still known as a relentless workaholic among his rivals. (It was said that he had a limousine built with three telephones that would whisk him away every morning to his office).

In an interview with the American television network C-SPAN, author and journalist James Stewart described Boesky in this way:

"He'll go to a restaurant, and a waiter would come by with the specials of the day...he'll have all of them – every special on the menu – eight, nine, ten – it didn't make a difference. They would have to wheel a whole separate table with all the dishes on it. He would circle the table and taste each dish – pick one and send all the rest back – paying for all of them. Money was not an object."[10]

Not only was money not an object, but the obsession of the dollar, he felt, was perfectly reasonable. In a commencement speech to the University of California, Berkeley graduates, he claimed that "Greed is all right...I think Greed is healthy. You can still be greedy and feel good about yourself." (This line, of course, was dramatized in Oliver Stones' *Wall*

---

[10] https://www.youtube.com/watch?v=D82Vy1NO-3I

Street a year later.) As the profitability of investing in takeover targets soared, the appetite for knowing what company was about to be picked also grew. In other words, the competition in the industry created a demand for inside information – something that was illegal. Also known as insider trading, it involves trading a company's stock or other securities by individuals with access to confidential or non-public information about the company. By law, it is illegal to profit from potential stock changes as it disadvantages public stockholders such as pension funds, investment banks, and insurance companies. It also betrays investors' trust, which is vital to the stock market's health.

Already predisposed toward making money – and lots of it- insider trading seemed almost inevitable for Boesky. And to help him – or so he thought, was one Dennis Levine. Born August 1, 1952, in Queens, New York, Levine was part of a tight-knit family where his father, Philip Levine, owned a small construction firm that sold aluminium and vinyl siding. The youngest of three boys, Levine helped his dad find new customers by doing door-to-door sales. Despite the rejections, the young New Yorker found a unique talent for selling and would not take no for an answer. He began studying the stock market when he was Thirteen and used some of the money he earned from helping his dad – around a hundred dollars initially- and invested them in stocks. By the time he reached the eighth grade, he was a regular reader of *The Wall Street Journal*. [11]

He lived with his parents until his mid-twenties when he decided to set his sights on earning millions as a businessman. Graduating with an MBA from CUNY's Baruch College, Levine was one of the "two or three most impressive students in his class," according to Leonard Larkin, a College's law department member at the time. After starting at Citicorp (now known as Citigroup), the New Yorker soon moved on to Smith Barney Harris Upham & Co. as an associate in 1978. The firm sent him to Paris for a year, where he and his wife Laurie lived it up in the company's state-of-the-art apartment on Avenue Foch (the first time they had been abroad). The two had met while she was attending College in New York City. [12] They would often ride the back roads of Long Island on his motorcycle,

---

11

https://www.washingtonpost.com/archive/lifestyle/1986/05/22/the-puzzling-wall-street-saga-of-dennis-levine/25e0b3ea-4038-4ce0-a3c2-edc2e111a181/

12

https://books.google.co.uk/books/about/Inside_Out.html?id=2Adz64snvg0C&redir_esc=y

dreaming of the day they'd marry once Dennis had finished his master's degree. She told *New York Magazine* that she vividly recalls her parents telling her she was the "girl who made good," having married a wealthy, handsome stockbroker. Her family, like Levine's, was Jewish and entrepreneurial. Laurie's first-generation European immigrant father owned several service stations near Manhattan.

To his surprise, Levine learned during their time in France that insider trading was legal in most European countries. Some executives told him that it was just a perk of the business –they made fun of American tax and securities laws, which were to them too stringent. He learned, too, that many of them were parking the cash they got from insider trading in bank accounts in Switzerland, Liechtenstein, and Luxembourg, where authorities strictly enforce bank secrecy laws. So Levine decided to open one too, borrowing as much as he could from his credit account and his family, selling them on the idea that he had found some lucrative investment opportunities. He would wait until he returned to the firm's New York office to start trading on inside information. Working out of the bank's mergers division, Levine gained access to non-public information, so he learned of transactions long before they were announced. To avoid getting caught by authorities, he opened a bank account in the Bahamian subsidiary of Bank Leu, Switzerland's oldest, under the code name "Mr. Diamond."

As Levine started to trade in more significant volumes, his circle of sources also grew. This was helped because he was the breaking news coordinator, meaning he closely monitored developments in the market and kept an eye on the famous Dow Jones ticker. Despite being promoted to second vice president, Levine left the bank in 1981 to go to Lehman Brothers Kuhn Loeb, which was a private partnership and a significant player in the mergers and acquisitions market. Within three years, he rose to senior vice president. However, his hopes of making a partner were dashed when Shearson/American Express acquired the bank a few years later. Not long afterwards, he was offered an opportunity as a managing director (the equivalent of partner) at Drexel – something he had long sought after at Lehman. Building on a string of successes a few months after his arrival, he was handed a bonus of well over **$1 million** in his first year. And it was during his first Drexel high-yield bond conference that he met Boesky. The

"Predators Ball"[13] was the investment bank's annual convention designed to match high-risk companies with investors who wanted high rewards. By the mid-80s, however, the conference became increasingly focused on setting up leveraged buyouts and hostile takeovers using junk bonds.

Flying Levine home with his private jet, the two struck a relationship and soon started trading information about deals. It is believed that Boesky used inside information from Levine to buy or hold at least seven stocks that were subject to takeovers. These included Nabisco Brands, American Natural Resources, Union Carbide, and General Foods.[14] Levine turned an initial investment of $39,750 into a profit of $11.5 million between 1980 and 1985 by trading stocks illegally based on inside information, according to the U.S. Securities and Exchange Commission (SEC) - the government agency responsible for regulating the securities market and protecting investors. He was soon arrested by US authorities in 1986 and later pleaded guilty to federal

---

[13] https://www.newsweek.com/wall-street-greed-apart-204816

[14] https://www.latimes.com/archives/la-xpm-1986-12-01-fi-11-story.html#:~:text=In%20addition%20to%20tipping%20Boesky,or%20were%20undertaking%20takeover%20defenses.

criminal charges related to insider trading. He agreed to give up more than $10.5 million in trading profits to settle a related civil suit brought by the SEC. In his book, "Inside Out," Levine explains how he became addicted to insider trading. "It was just so easy. In seven years, I built $39,750 into $11.5 million, and all it took was a 20-second phone call to my offshore bank a couple of times a month -- maybe 200 calls total. My account was growing at 125% a year, compounded. Believe me; I felt a rush when I would check the price of one of my stocks on the office Quotron and learn I'd just made several hundred thousand dollars. I was confident that the elaborate veils of secrecy I had created -- plus overseas bank privacy laws -- would protect me."[15]

As part of Levine's plea, he agreed to work with prosecutors to give up information on other Wall Street professionals, including Ivan Boesky, with whom he believed to have traded stocks on inside information. He, too, was arrested by the SEC – who charged that from February 1985, he had profited from illegal stock tips.

---

[15] https://www.upi.com/Archives/1990/05/01/Admitted-insider-trader-says-practice-was-addiction/3671641534400/

News of Boesky's arrest rocked Wall Street because, for more than a decade, he had been the Street's lead speculator when it came to trading takeover stocks, so much so that he became a significant factor in the takeover market, often affecting how transactions in the M&A market would often shake out. Boesky would agree to pay $100 million to the SEC - $50 million for his illegal profits and a further $50 million fine (the most significant penalty at the time). He was also barred from the U.S. securities industry and pleaded guilty to federal felony charges. He, too, agreed to cooperate with officials in their ongoing investigations into illegal trading.

With the help of Levine and Boesky, the SEC built a case against other names on Wall Street – including perhaps one of the biggest - Michael Milken – head of the high-yield bond department at Drexel Burnham.

Known as "the Oral Roberts of junk bonds" and "Milken the Magnificent" - Milken epitomized Greed during the 1980s[16]. Born in Encino, California, in 1946, he attended Birmingham High School – graduating in 1964, before

---

[16] https://www.latimes.com/archives/la-xpm-1987-08-30-tm-5066-story.html

studying at the University of California at Berkeley. In 1969, a year after his graduation, he began working at the banking firm Drexel Firestone while he was studying at the University of Pennsylvania's Wharton School of Finance. [17]It was there where Milken began research on the untapped market of high-yield bonds – also known as "junk bonds." He saw that the big credit agencies, such as Standard & Poor's and Moody's, were downgrading the bonds of once-great blue-chip corporations that were going through tough times. Dubbed "Fallen Angels," these bonds were seen as risky investments because they had gone from AAA (investment grade) to C-grade ('junk') status. Milken, however, concluded that these bonds were under-priced and, despite their higher interest rates – were worth the risk and would create opportunities to make big profits because the rating agencies, he believed, were using the wrong criteria (past performance) to assign their ratings. Not only that, but Milken saw the use of junk bonds as a way to open up a corporate bond market (valued at around $800 billion at the time), which had previously been restricted to about 600 to 700 companies. Suddenly, with the supply of high-yield

---

[17] https://www.britannica.com/biography/Michael-R-Milken

bonds, institutions with unfavourable credit ratings would have access to capital.

David Boies, a superb litigator and co-founder of law firm Boies Schiller Flexner, would tell the finance publication *Business Insider* that Milken "revolutionized the way companies — in particular, companies involved in corporate transactions — were financed...He changed that fundamentally. If you look at the way companies were financed, there is a 'before Michael Milken' and an 'after Michael Milken.'"[18]

When Drexel Firestone merged with Burnham & Company to form Drexel Burnham Lambert Inc. in 1971[19], Milken approached the investment bank's hierarchy about creating and heading up a high-yield bond department where he could take advantage of his findings. And boy, he did. By 1976, Milen was earning 100% of the capital that the bank provided him with. Soon enough, he was one of Drexel's important figures - moving its high-yield bond department

---

18

https://www.institutionalinvestor.com/article/2bsvz8m3fr9zbx7r0b9c0/corner-office/the-michael-milken-project

[19] https://www.nytimes.com/1973/02/03/archives/wall-st-houses-planning-merger-burnham-co-and-drexel-firestone-to.html

from New York to Los Angeles in 1978 and later to the opulent Gump's department store building in Beverly Hills. "Drexel became this white-hot magnet...The real financial power centre was the high-yield floor and the guys who worked for Milken. A lot of really smart people figured that out, and they gravitated toward Los Angeles," said former Drexel alumni Peter Nolan in an interview with *The Los Angeles Times*. [20]The bank underwrote its first junk bond in April 1977 when it raised $30 million for the oil exploration company Texas International. Half a dozen more deals were done by the end of the year – totalling $124.5 million. The following year, the total soared to $439.5 million – more than doubling the amount of deals compared to the year before. With the help of Milken, Drexel instantly grabbed over 70 per cent of the junk bond market, beating out its main rival, Lehman Brothers – who were facing a turbulent power struggle between its two partners, Peter G. Peterson and Lewis L. Glucksman.

Not content with its dominance in the junk bond market, Drexel dipped its toe into the leveraged buyout market. In its basic form, a leveraged buyout (LBO) is a transaction in

---

[20] https://www.latimes.com/business/la-fi-milken-drexel-legacy-20160501-story.html

which private investors borrow money to purchase a corporation or a corporate division (Palepu, 1990). These investors are usually either the current management of the target company, a single or a group of private equity firms, or third-party investors. Their goal is to grab a share of the company, purchasing all outstanding shares of the company, putting up five to ten per cent of the purchase price from their own money, and borrowing the rest—hence the term "leverage." Milken saw that he could use junk bonds to finance these buyouts – moreover, he knew it was the perfect time to pounce. (It's estimated that there were over 2,000 LBOs between 1979 and 1989 – totalling around $250 billion). [21] Atop the LBO industry were the private equity giants Kohlberg Kravis Roberts & Co., which Henry Kravis and George R. Roberts ran. Despite their success, the cousins noticed that the need to access cash became vital as the corporate takeover field began to get crowded. Hence, KKR found a powerful new partner in Milken who could raise large sums of money by selling "junk" bonds. In 1984, they completed their first deal together when KKR needed to stump up an extra $100 million for the buyout of the retailing

---

21

https://www.ecgi.global/sites/default/files/working_papers/documents/SSRN-id2896653.pdf

company Cole National. Through Milken's magic, he convinced several investors to come up with the cash in a meeting at the firm's office in Beverly Hills. It began a lucrative partnership culminating in one of the largest and most talked about LBOs of all time – when KKR bought the massive tobacco and consumer products company RJR Nabisco for almost $25 billion in 1989. The deal which made daily headlines in the financial press (*Time Magazine* once went with the headline: "*A Game of Greed.*") [22], was considered by many as the height of Greed in Corporate America. Milken's firm played a crucial role in the transaction, raising an estimated $6 billion. The California native received plaudits from all quarters, with one *Washington Post* columnist saying he "helped create the conditions for America's explosion of wealth and creativity." This was reflected in his pay packet, which topped $550 million in 1987, making the Guinness Book of World Records as the largest sum of money earned in a single year. But while The Economist was lauding him for fueling much of America's economic growth, others weren't so complimentary and found his earnings hard to stomach. "It's

---

[22] https://content.time.com/time/magazine/0,9263,7601881205,00.html

embarrassing to our financial system," Samuel L. Hayes, a professor of investment banking at the Harvard Business School, once said. "It portrays the image of an industry that has gotten totally out of control in terms of its greed for money, " he continued.[23]

However, it wouldn't be too long before Milken's reign began to crumble. On September 7, 1988, the SEC filed an 184-page civil lawsuit against Drexel and four employees– including Wall Street's junk bond king. [24]The lawsuit, the most sweeping fraud case at the time, charged that the firm committed a host of securities law violations, including illegally trading on insider information and manipulating stock prices. It was alleged that in 1986, Drexel received a $5.3 million payment from the Boesky to balance profits and losses from a secret arrangement they had with the Detroit native. The suit claimed this was done to hide the fact that the firm was trading based on confidential information about upcoming corporate takeovers. Altogether, Sixteen

---

[23] https://www.nytimes.com/1989/04/03/business/wages-even-wall-st-can-t-stomach.html

[24] https://www.nytimes.com/1988/09/08/business/drexel-burnham-charged-by-sec-with-stock-fraud.html

transactions took place between both parties. Drexel quickly denied the claim, saying in a statement that:

"We believe, based on the information available to us, that the charges filed by the SEC are wrong. After an examination of 1.5 million pages of documentation and interviews of scores of Drexel Burnham employees, we continue to believe that neither Drexel Burnham nor any of our employees named in this matter have engaged in any wrongdoing. We expect to be vindicated."

On Boesky, who had helped authorities in their investigations, they said:

"The evidence indicates that this fee was payment for normal corporate finance, research, and other advisory services furnished to the Boesky organization prior to March 1986... Indeed, Ivan Boesky's allegations must be viewed in the context in which they were made: Boesky was desperate to settle with the SEC and to minimize his own punishment by accusing others. We are particularly eager to confront

Ivan Boesky in the fair and open forum of a court to demonstrate that his charges are false."[25]

Despite its pleas of innocence, Drexel reached a deal a few months later to pay the government $650 million to settle the civil and criminal charges filed by the government. As for Milken, he was indicted with 98 counts of fraud, racketeering, and insider trading by Federal officials in the spring of 1989. He's said to have yielded $1.85 billion from 1984 to 1986 due to his illegal schemes. The charges resulted from the federal government's most intensive criminal securities fraud investigations. He was sentenced to Ten years in prison, which included Three years of probation and 5,400 hours of community service. "Your crimes show a pattern of skirting the law, stepping just over to the wrong side of the law in an apparent effort to get some of the benefits from violating the law without running a substantial risk of being caught," said U.S. District Judge Kimba Wood. "Milken is a symbol of the 1980s," said Samuel Hayes, an investment banking professor at the Harvard Business School. "He created something in the junk bond and built it

---

[25] https://www.sechistorical.org/collection/papers/1980/1988_0907_DrexelSECSuitT.pdf

into an extraordinarily powerful machine. In retrospect, it now appears that some of the momentum behind that machine was due to illegal actions."

Milken's arrest and subsequent sentencing was the curtain call on what people called a "decade of greed." [26]The crimes of his co-conspirators put a pin in what was Wall Street's coming out party as years of excessive and extravagance came to a dramatic halt. Deal-making slowed down, and so did the big bonuses and editorial exposure. However, this was just a short respite for an industry that was about to be much bigger through the 90s and 2000s and find ever more innovative ways of becoming greedier.

---
[26]

https://www.nationalaffairs.com/storage/app/uploads/public/58e/1a4/e06/58e1a4e06b677616501656.pdf

"Fraud is the daughter of greed."

-Dr. John Grant

Accounting for Greed

WHY DO THE rich want to be so rich? Why did money get to mean so much in our society? How did nice guys come, in the '70s and '80s, to behave in increasingly selfish and greedy ways? [27]That was what one columnist mused following the insider trading scandals of the 1980s. The adoration of riches was not a new phenomenon then; in the mid-to-late 19th century came the Gilded Age — a term American writer and entrepreneur Mark Twain coined in 1873 — which offered equally flamboyant displays of wealth. But it's fair to say that the world attaches far more significance to money than God ever intended. Instead of being an avenue for people to trade goods and services and thus a medium of exchange, it has become an object of status, happiness, and security. For some, gratitude is their

---

[27] https://www.latimes.com/archives/la-xpm-1990-06-14-vw-474-story.html

natural response to good fortune, especially if it has come from hard work.

For others, they become possessed by restlessness and an insatiable spirit, and their response is to want even more money. Such people become so fixated on the object of their greed and wish to accumulate and hoard as much as possible at whatever cost. Dennis Levine, whom we discussed in our previous chapter, was a case in point – admitting that his ambition was so great that he lost all rationality. "I gradually lost sight of what constitutes ethical behaviour," he said. "At each new level of success, I set higher goals, imprisoning myself in a cycle from which I saw no escape. When I became a senior vice president, I wanted to be a managing director, and when I became a managing director, I wanted to be a client. If I was making $100,000 a year, I thought I could make $200,000. And if I made $1 million, I can make $3 million." [28]

You can call it greed, avarice, or covetousness – either way, it's one of the strongest desires that can grip the heart of a human being. You might even call it the ultimate addiction.

---

[28]

https://money.cnn.com/magazines/fortune/fortune_archive/1990/05/21/73553/index.htm\

And what's worse (though this isn't always the case) is that those typically thirsty for wealth aren't in the professions or creative arts. It's those who are in business and finance, i.e., entrepreneurs, investors, speculators, lenders, and CEOs. By nature, they are highly competitive and aggressive, ruthlessly taking advantage of every opportunity to turn a profit—in some cases, doing it illegally. And, If you thought insider trading was one thing, the corporate accounting scandals in the late 1990s were just as bad – and revealed that despite the jail sentences handed down to Milken and Co., greed in Corporate America never went away – in fact, it grew even bigger.

The biggest accounting scandal centred around Enron. On October 16, 2001, Enron stunned Wall Street by announcing that it had a $618 million net loss for the third quarter and would reduce shareholder equity by $1.2 billion. Once the seventh largest company in the U.S. - reporting billions in revenues and boasting of political connections on Capitol Hill in Washington D.C., the company went bankrupt. It was the poster child of an era of corporate greed and corruption. It had gone from trading at $90 a share in the mid-2000s to 45 cents a share by the time it collapsed 18 months later. For half a decade, its CEOs Kenneth Lay and Jeffrey Skilling had convinced shareholders and the business world alike that it was one of America's greatest success stories. Indeed, *Fortune Magazine* declared it the most "innovative company" in Corporate America[29] six years in a row. It donated money to political campaigns (both Democrats and Republicans). It was on its way to being America's biggest company, given that it had built a business that combined gas, energy, broadband, and commodities trading. The company could do no wrong in the eyes of its admires.

Formed in 1985 following the merger of two gas companies, Houston Natural Gas and InterNorth, Enron was originally a gas pipeline company based in Houston, Texas. But just as it was building up ahead of steam, the U.S. Congress adopted a series of laws to deregulate the sale of natural gas in the early 1990s. [30] As a result, the company lost its exclusive right to operate its pipelines and was exposed to greater competition. Therefore, CEO Kenneth Lay had to devise a strategy to survive in a more competitive market. And to do that, he had to hire someone with the smarts. That someone

---

[29] https://link.springer.com/chapter/10.1057/9780230518865_12

30 https://www.jec.senate.gov/reports/97th%20Congress/Natural%20Gas%20Deregulation%20(1138).pdf

was a young consultant named Jeffrey Skilling, whose work at the global consultancy giant Mckinsey & Co. had impressed him. A Harvard graduate with an MBA from the university's business school, Skilling was just the lieutenant Lay needed. Graduating in the top 5% of his class, he once said in an interview that he was "****** smart." [31]

When he joined the company, he thought that digging and supplying pipelines for oil and gas was on the wane and believed that Enron should move into the future and instead go into the business of buying and selling energy. As such, he was given the green light to start a "Gas Bank"- which would trade natural gas just as one would trade any other financial commodity such as stocks, bonds, and currencies. Soon enough, Enron raced up the corporate ladder – making profits and becoming the world's most prominent energy trader, thus turning its two CEOs into global rock stars. Not content with the energy business, Skilling set his sights on another profit-making scheme: Broadband Telecommunications. They came up with providing internet services while trading rights to broadband capacity. They called it Enron Broadband Services – a business Skilling

---

[31] https://www.alumni.hbs.edu/stories/Pages/story-bulletin.aspx?num=726

thought could add $40 billion to the company's market value. The announcement that it was leaping into telecommunications caused an immediate bounce in its share price.

However, despite its deal with the video and DVD chain Blockbuster, its bandwidth trading initiative failed within a few years of its creation. Although the venture didn't create much revenue for the firm (in fact, it was making losses by the end), the fact that Enron became bigger and bigger meant that investors, journalists, and market watchers were taking more notice. This was crucial to the firm's fate as its ever-increasing exposure illuminated how it had valued its assets. Approved by the SEC in 1992, Enron had moved from the traditional historical cost accounting method to what's known as the mark-to-market (MTM) [32]accounting method. Simply put, MTM involves recording the value of an asset to reflect its current market levels. [33]At the end of the fiscal year, a company's annual financial statements must reflect the current market value of its accounts. It's considered a good way of valuing assets as it provides a

---

[32] https://www.govinfo.gov/content/pkg/CPRT-107SPRT82147/html/CPRT-107SPRT82147.htm

[33] https://core.ac.uk/reader/234631270

realistic appraisal of an institution's current financial situation and is widely used by many businesses. Enron's use of this practice was scrutinized as some started believing it was cooking its books. "People who raise questions are people who have not gone through [our business] in detail and who want to throw rocks at us,"[34] Skilling was once quoted as saying in an article by Bethany McLean of *Fortune Magazine*.[35] (McLean and fellow fortune journalist Peter Elkind would later chronicle the rise and fall of the company in *The Smartest Guys in the Room*). But sure enough, its top executives had abused the MTM accounting practice that Enron used and opened the door for fraud and deception.

In 2001, it admitted that it had overstated profits from 1997 by $600m, causing the SEC to investigate its finances. By then, Skilling had already quit as CEO, and Enron was losing money by the day. As it entered the last month of 2001, it filed for bankruptcy, making it the biggest in US history at

---

[34] https://money.cnn.com/magazines/fortune/fortune_archive/2001/12/24/315319/index.htm

[35] https://fortune.com/2015/12/30/is-enron-overpriced-fortune-2001/

the time.[36] Thousands of employees lost their jobs and life savings. Soon after, the Justice Department opened criminal investigations into its business practices. Although it took four years, Skilling and its founder - Ken Lay, were found guilty of conspiracy and fraud. Skilling was found guilty on 19 counts of conspiracy, fraud, false statements, and insider trading, while Lay was found guilty on all six counts of conspiracy and fraud. The 12-team jury concluded that the former executives had misled the public about Enron's true financial health. "We were the icon of America. [37]

It is the seventh largest company in the world, and Ken Lay brought it to that. It was because of him. Greed took over. These guys were rich, and they just wanted to get richer and richer," said former employee Angelina Lairo. Andrew Fastow, who was their clever numbers guy and chief financial officer, admitted to the Houston jury that he was "extremely greedy" and had "lost my moral compass." [38]

---

[36] http://news.bbc.co.uk/1/hi/business/1688550.stm

[37] https://abcnews.go.com/Business/LegalCenter/story?id=2003728&page=1

[38] https://www.theguardian.com/business/2006/mar/09/corporatefraud.enron

It wasn't just Fastow who had lost his moral compass; most of Wall Street had. In testimony before Congress, Federal Reserve Chairman Alan Greenspan spoke of this greed as "infectious" not long after Enron's collapse:

"An infectious greed seemed to grip much of our business community...Too many corporate executives sought ways to "harvest" some of those stock market gains. As a result, the highly desirable spread of shareholding and options among business managers perversely created incentives to artificially inflate reported earnings in order to keep stock prices high and rising. This outcome suggests that the options were poorly structured, and, consequently, they failed to properly align the long-term interests of shareholders and managers, the paradigm so essential for effective corporate governance. The incentives they created overcame the good judgment of too many corporate managers. It is not that humans have become any more greedy than in generations past. It is that the avenues to express greed had grown so enormously."[39]

---

[39] https://www.federalreserve.gov/boarddocs/hh/2002/july/testimony.htm

At the time, it was widely believed that the Enron scandal was an outliner. A rare blip in a decade deplete of any major scandal on Wall Street and Corporate America. But, it soon became apparent that this was anything but an isolated case of financial accounting fraud at a major corporation. Enron's record largest bankruptcy in United States history was soon eclipsed by WorldCom, whose less sophisticated accounting fraud led to a larger restatement of earnings, a larger bankruptcy filing, and equally far-reaching civil and criminal investigations. The story began in 1983 when the break-up of the multinational telecommunications giant AT&T left a gap in the long-distance telephone market. [40]Sensing an opportunity, a group of men, including businessman Murray Waldron and William Rector, met in a coffee shop in Jacksonville, Mississippi. [41]What would come out of the meeting was the Long Distance Discount Service (LDDS), which would later become WorldCom. One of the men in the meeting was Bernard Ebbers. Described by one person as a "stern" but a "hard worker," little did he know that this small venture would catapult him

---

40 https://historyofcomputercommunications.info/section/1.5/institutional-change-in-communications-deregulation-and-break-up-of-at&t/

[41] https://www.academia.edu/5419693/World_Com_Case

into being one of the wealthiest men in America. Bernie's business model was simple - WorldCom didn't build landline cables or cell phone towers but would instead rent out this infrastructure from other companies. The expense was called "Line Cost." Using this existing infrastructure, WorldCom would offer customers cell phones and landline services at a discounted rate. The hope was that this customer income would be enough to offset any expenses from renting out the landlines. The companies' first years were rough. Until 1985, they made losses repeatedly as the company went into debt of $1.5 million[42]. At this point, the owners decided to hand over the reins to Ebbers, making him the president and Chief Executive Officer (CEO). Ebbers was somewhat of a nobody before becoming a CEO. Born in 1941 in Edmonton, Canada, he was the son of a travelling salesman who relocated his family to the US. He attended school on a Navajo reservation in New Mexico, returning to Canada to work as a bouncer and milkman. This didn't last long, as he became a basketball coach before cutting his teeth in the motel business, where he owned a chain of 9

---

[42] https://www.youtube.com/watch?v=u_rfIboPyYs&t=613s

motels.[43] He was well known as someone who would save every penny he received during that time. He would personally clean and change each bedroom in the motel complex instead of paying someone else to do it. Now the CEO at WorldCom, he was ruthless in his efforts to gain profits and started to count the costs immediately – including cutting out the company's free coffee policy.

Even though some felt that the penny-pinching was going too far, his efforts ensured a revenue rise in the first few months at the helm. In 1986, revenue rose to $8.6 million, and a year later grew to $18 million. Despite this, the competition in the market was still challenging because multiple companies were providing the same service.[44] To grow rapidly, Bernie embarked on a different strategy: acquiring regional rivals or merging with its competitors. 1995, for instance, WorldCom acquired voice and data transmission company Williams Telecommunications Group Inc. (WilTel) for $2.5 billion cash. Indeed, the firm acquired close to 30 companies in the years following its existence. Its sales reached $1 billion when it officially

---

[43] https://www.nytimes.com/2020/02/03/business/bernard-ebbers-dead.html

[44] https://www.youtube.com/watch?v=u_rflboPyYs&t=613s

became WorldCom Inc. in 1995. Its largest merger occurred in 1998 when it outbid British telecoms giant BT and merged with MCI Communications- a company twice its size. The $40 billion dollar merger, finalized on September 15, 1998, was heralded as "the largest corporate merger in history" by the Los Angeles Times.

It completed a hat-trick of mergers for WorldCom, merging with the US local phone provider Brooks Fibre Properties Inc. ($1.2 billion) and the online service provider CompuServe Corp. ($1.3 billion). Furthermore, a year later, it was close to creating a telecoms mammoth when it proposed to merge with rival U.S telecoms giant Sprint Inc. for an estimated deal of [45]$129 billion. However, the deal fell apart when the U.S. Justice Department recommended against it because it would combine the second-largest and third-largest long-distance carriers, and the two companies would dominate Internet switching services – thus violating antitrust laws. The DOJ lawsuit said: "For millions of residential and business customers throughout the nation, the

---

[45] https://www.verizon.com/about/news/worldcom-and-mci-announce-37-billion-merger

merger will lead to higher prices, lower service quality, and less innovation."

Janet Reno, the US attorney general at the time, said: "This merger threatens to undermine the competitive gains achieved since the [justice] department challenged AT&T's monopoly of the telecommunications industry 25 years ago." [46] In other words - the group would become a monopoly at the expense of consumers, who would have to pay exorbitant prices due to the reduced competitive environment.

Nevertheless, WorldCom didn't show any signs of slowing down. By 2000, WorldCom employed 88,000 employees and owned 60,000 miles of telephone line - not just in the U.S. but worldwide. Its revenue would eventually cross $40 billion, and its stock price was skyrocketing by the minute. At the peak of the tech bubble, WorldCom had a market cap of $186bn, giving Ebbers an estimated fortune of $1.4bn.

---

[46] https://www.justice.gov/archive/atr/public/press_releases/2000/5049.htm

Ebbers soon becomes somewhat of a renegade hero on Wall Street- primarily due to his casual dress sense and salesman attitude – even calling himself the "telecoms Cowboy."

By this stage, Bernie was receiving stock options of over $27 million from his firm. Stock options are financial instruments that provide individuals the right to buy a specific number of company shares at a predetermined price within a specified timeframe. To fund his lavish lifestyle, he would take out loans from JPMorgan and secure them with WorldCom stock. According to a report by CNBC, $408 million was taken out of the company to pay for the purchase of yachts and then a yacht-building company - not to mention the purchase of the biggest ranch on earth - Douglas Lake Ranch. Ebbers soon resigned amid the SEC's probe of the company's support of more than $400 million in personal loans. It marked a stunning fall from grace not just for Ebbers but also for the Mississippi telecoms giant – whose stock price at the time had plummeted to $2.35, having topped out above $64 a share three years earlier in 1999.[47]

---

[47] https://www.nytimes.com/2002/11/05/business/corporate-loans-used-personally-report-discloses.html

The rejected merger with Sprint by regulators did, however, sow the seeds for fraud at the company as it exhausted its ability to grow through mergers and acquisitions. Even though the internet was gaining traction, the long-distance telecommunications cash cow seemed to be drying up. Being in the infrastructure game wasn't as profitable as it once was. This was compounded when the tech bubble burst in 2000, which hit the telecom industry hard. This led to desperation amongst WorldCom's ranks: its head accountant, David Meyers, brought critical financial documents to its then CFO Scott Sullivan, who would baulk at the lack of company profits. He thought there must have been a mistake - so he sent Myers back to look at the report.

However, the accounting department returned with the same number - to Sullivan- but the figures didn't add up. Sullivan knew this wouldn't be good for the company as it was plc and the earnings report soon. If the company were to report its current earnings - it would be at the mercy of investors, who would send their share even lower (it was hovering around $18 at the time). Out of desperation, Sullivan instructed Myers to write down (make) financial entries. At first, he thought everything would be figured out by the next earnings season so that it wouldn't be an issue. [48]

When the next quarter came around, he instructed David to do the same; the next quarter, he did the same again. Realizing that just making game entries wasn't going to be enough to make the margins look impressive- he told Myers to do something more fraudulent - he would take the costs of renting cell and landline infrastructure and hook them down as assets this was to make WorldCom appear to be in a financially healthy and stable posting to shareholders and investors. This was illegal as these were expenses rather than assets supposed to generate income.

Glyn Smith, a high-ranking executive within WorldCom's internal audit division, collaborated closely with the Vice President of Audit, Cynthia Cooper. Together, they conducted an in-depth investigation into WorldCom's capital expenditures and capital accounts.

They discovered WorldCom's inappropriate categorization of line charges as capital investments during their findings. As a result, WorldCom was forced to revise its previously

---

[48] https://www.youtube.com/watch?v=u_rflboPyYs&t=613s

reported expenses for 2001, increasing them by a staggering $3.01 billion. Additionally, they prompted the company to adjust its first-quarter expenses for 2002, raising them by $800 million. It didn't take longer than a few months for Sullivan to be fired. [49]"As a result of an internal audit of the company's capital expenditure accounting, it was determined that certain transfers from line cost expenses to capital accounts during this period were not made by generally accepted accounting principles," the company said. The company has also accepted the resignation of David Myers.

And so, following a slew of resignations at the top of the organization, a plunging share price, and intense scrutiny from auditors and the SEC, WorldCom eventually filed for Chapter 11 bankruptcy protection in July of 2002 - nearly one month after it revealed that it had improperly booked $3.8 billion in expenses. Crippled by debts north of $41 billion and assets of $107 billion, WorldCom's bankruptcy is the largest in United States history, dwarfing that of Enron Corp. (The Houston-based energy trader listed $63.4 billion in assets when it filed Chapter 11 a year prior.) Thousands of WorldCom employees lost their jobs as a result.[50] Ebbers

---

[49] https://www.cfo.com/news/the-view-from-the-inside/681764/

[50] http://news.bbc.co.uk/1/hi/business/2143217.stm

was convicted in March 2005 on nine felony counts for his role in WorldCom's $11 billion fraud and was sentenced to 25 years in prison. In addition to his prison sentence, he agreed to forfeit most of his assets, worth as much as $45 million, which were used to pay some of the people and entities impacted by the fraud.

So rather than greed being good and causing the upward surge of humanity, it was the gateway for crime and dishonesty – ultimately leading to jail sentences, job losses, and suicide (former Enron vice chairman J. Clifford Baxter was found dead in his Mercedes during the height of the criminal investigations). Melanie Klein, the Austrian-British psychoanalyst, claimed that the prospect of death makes people "greedy for life," so they strive to accumulate as much as they can for themselves before the "game is up." She called this the "death drive."[51]

How ironic, then, that one can gain all the wealth that they could imagine – yet not be around to spend it when they die. Perhaps that's why, in the Bible, Jesus Christ warns us against the "least bit of greed," as he believes that our life should not consist of the possessions that we have.

---

[51] https://hbr.org/2003/02/i-was-greedy-too

He illustrates this (as he often did) in a parable called "The Rich Fool," which can be found in the 12th Chapter of the Gospel according to Luke:

"A rich man had a fertile farm that produced fine crops. **17** In fact, his barns were full to overflowing—he couldn't get everything in. He thought about his problem, **18**, and finally exclaimed, 'I know—I'll tear down my barns and build bigger ones! Then I'll have enough room. **19** And I'll sit back and say to myself, "Friend, you have enough stored away for years to come. Now, take it easy! Wine, women, and song for you!"'[d]

20 "But God said to him, 'Fool! Tonight, you die. Then who will get it all?'

21 "Yes, every man is a fool who gets rich on earth but not in heaven."

Jesus told this parable in response to a man who had wished to settle a dispute over his estate with his brother because he felt that he hadn't been given a fair share of the family inheritance. (Back then, rabbis often served as mediators in such disputes.) However, Jesus wanted to have no part of it, and instead uses the illustration of the rich farmer to explain why we shouldn't set our hearts on earthly possessions because, as Adam Clarke once wrote, "Great possessions are generally accompanied with pride, idleness, and luxury; and these are the greatest enemies to salvation." In the parable, the farmer's pride and luxury made him idle – he thought he could take it easy with no care in the world.

Then, out of nowhere, the game was up for him. He embodies having gained the whole world but lost his soul. His greed had made him prioritize the wrong thing. As such, he was considered a "fool" because of this. Moreover, the writer of Ecclesiastes notes that "Wisdom and money can get you almost anything," but only wisdom can save our lives. So rather than choosing to be wise and rich towards the things of God, this farmer thought money could be his defence – and that was his downfall. Indeed, earlier in the Gospels, Jesus uses an interesting metaphor to forewarn us against stockpiling wealth:

"Don't hoard treasure down here where it gets eaten by moths and corroded by rust or—worse! stolen by burglars. Stockpile treasure in heaven, where it's safe from moth and rust and burglars." (Matthew 6:19-20 MSG)

He goes on to say that where our treasure is – that's where our heart will be also. And so having money in the centre of our hearts is a dangerous place to be. You may have heard of the saying, "Money is the root of all evil."

However, the actual quote is that the "*love* of money is the root of all evil." The love of money causes people to fall into temptation and commit evil deeds – whether white-collar crimes – like accounting fraud and insider trading or blue-collar crimes such as robbery and theft. The Apostle Paul – the one responsible for the line, even says that some religious leaders of his day had "wandered from the true faith and pierced themselves with many sorrows" because of greed. Perhaps that's why the writer of the Book of Hebrews tells us that we should keep our lives "free" from the love of money and be content with what we have.

Paul knew this more than anyone because, as he explains in the Book Philippians, he knew the secret of being content (the opposite of greedy) – having experienced being both rich and having plenty – and being poor and hungry. In other words, living at both extremes had created a sense of contentment that meant he never had an outsized desire to hunt for more than he already had.

Unfortunately, that same contentment was missing from the individuals outlined in the last two chapters. Despite having used their skills and education to earn wealth legally- the appetite to make even more money drove them to illegal practices – of which they were all eventually found out. As a result, they were either jailed, lost most of their wealth, or banned by their field.

So, if you thought greed was good, think again.

"The world's most powerful investment bank is a great vampire squid wrapped around the face of humanity, relentlessly jamming its blood funnel into anything that smells like money."

– Matt Taibbi.

Doing God's Work

AFTER SPENDING ALMOST 12 years at one of the world's biggest and most successful investment banks, Greg Smith decided enough was enough despite starting as a summer intern at its Stanford office and then moving to New York and then to London. He felt that the culture at the once great bank had become too toxic and destructive and that the bank had ditched its focus on the customer and instead focused its efforts on making the next buck. The trajectory of its culture had reached such a nadir that in his final year at the firm, he saw five different managing directors refer to their clients as "muppets," sometimes over internal email as they ripped off unsuspecting customers.

Indeed, the most common question he would get from junior analysts was, "How much money did we make off the client?" – highlighting the company's shift in identity. The company that Smith left was Goldman Sachs. [52]Celebrating its 150th year in existence at the beginning of 2019, the investment bank has been called many names for its perceived unethical behaviour. Nicknames such as Goldman Sucks, Goldmine Sacks, and Goldman Shafts have been used to describe the "Bad Boys" of Wall Street. But perhaps the best description of Goldman comes from Rolling Stones writer Matt Taibbi, who called the firm a "great vampire squid wrapped around the face of humanity, relentlessly jamming its blood funnel into anything that smells like money." It's the quote that perhaps best describes how the public felt about Goldman after the financial crisis of 2008.[53]

This hatred was crystallized by the U.S. Securities and Exchange Commission's case against ex-Goldman trader Fabrice Tourre, who had to pay more than $825,000 after he was found liable for defrauding institutional investors in a subprime mortgage product that he knew was doomed to

---

[52] https://www.nytimes.com/2012/03/14/opinion/why-i-am-leaving-goldman-sachs.html

[53] https://www.rollingstone.com/politics/politics-news/the-great-american-bubble-machine-195229/

fail.[54] The complex mortgage deal, Abacus 2007-AC1, cost investors $1bn (£661m). The Frenchman was found guilty of six fraud claims and was ordered to pay $650,000 in civil fines and give up an additional $175,463 bonus plus interest linked to the transaction. Described by the regulator as the "face of Wall Street greed," the trader called himself "Fabulous Fab."

The nickname epitomized corporate greed and vanity running amok when investors saw their savings diminish. "The whole building is about to collapse anytime now ... Only potential survivor, the fabulous Fab ... standing in the middle of all these complex, highly leveraged, exotic trades he created without necessarily understanding all of the implications of those monstruosities [sic]!!!" He wrote in an internal email seen by the SEC. At the time, SEC lawyer, Matthew Martens, said the investment Tourre arranged was "secretly designed to maximize the potential it would fail," he said. "In the end, Wall Street greed drove Mr. Tourre to lie and deceive." Goldman eventually settled with the SEC in 2010 by paying a $550 million fine. The firm, however, didn't admit or deny any wrongdoing.

---

[54] https://www.cnbc.com/2014/03/13/big-fine-imposed-on-ex-goldman-trader-tourre-in-sec-case.html

Things weren't always like this at Goldman. It was originally a family business that did not take deposits, issue credit cards, make mortgage loans, or interact with its clients. It was founded in 1869 by Marcus Goldman, who emigrated from Germany to New York in 1848 and was one of the first Jewish Immigrants to America.

Born in 1821 in the small village of Trappstadt in Grabfeld, he was the eldest son of five children. He moved across the States as a salesman, travelling via horse and cart, before reaching Philadelphia, where he invested in a sewing machine so that he would become a tailor. There, he met and married his wife, Bertha Goldmann, who, at 19, also emigrated to America from Bavaria in 1848 and was a practising sticker. They eventually set up a clothing store in Pennsylvania and, 20 years later, decided to move back to New York City with their five children. Goldman then set up shop as a banker in a one-bedroom apartment on Pine Street in Lower Manhattan and called the company Marcus Goldman & Co.

He did lucrative business with diamond dealers and could trade as much as $5 million worth of commercial paper annually. Commercial paper is a short-term loan as an IOU, which promises to pay the payee a certain amount. Big corporations often issue commercial paper to raise money – usually to pay for short-term debt payments. According to Nasdaq, "Short-term promissory notes are either unsecured or backed by assets such as loans or mortgages issued by a corporation. The maturity of commercial paper is typically less than 270 days."

It was said that Goldman would stuff commercial papers into his silk hat whenever he would travel to the Chemical Bank on Chambers Street, the Importers and Traders Bank on Warren Street, or the National City Bank on Wall Street. The "altitude" or thickness of a person's hat would indicate how successful someone has been during the day.

During this period, the Goldmans became good friends with Joseph and Sophia Sachs – who also emigrated from Germany. The friendship between the two families grew so much that Marcus's two daughters and Bertha married two sons of the Sachs family. The youngest daughter, Louisa, became the wife of Samuel Sachs, whom Marcus decided to add as a partner to his commercial paper business – having run it single-handily since its inception. This was the norm on the Street as firms all looked alike – small private partnerships that were run by families Goldman & Sachs – three Lehman brothers, Lizard brothers (Lizard). But as part of his inclusion as a partner, Sam had to sell his dry-goods business and take a $15,000 loan from his father-in-law, which had to be repaid in three years (which he did). By the time Sam had joined the firm in 1882, business was booming.

Two years prior, it was turning over as much as $30 million of commercial paper and had a capital of $100,000. It also won business from several midwestern companies, including Sears Roebuck, Cluett Peabody, and Rice-Stix Dry Goods. In 1885, Goldman added his son Henry and son-in-law Ludwig Dreyfuss as junior partners and Henry Sachs a year later. The firm would now become known as Goldman Sachs &. Co., and through its budding partnership, it succeeded in becoming the most prominent commercial paper dealer in the United States – and by 1896, it was listed on the New York Stock Exchange.

As the firm moved into the twentieth century, Henry embarked on a strategy to expand the business and set his sights on underwriting stocks in the railroad and utilities sectors, which were growing exponentially. However, the space was heavily dominated by rival investment houses J. P. Morgan & Co., Kuhn, Loeb & Co., and Speyer & Co. Not only did these firms dominate the market, but he also knew they would aggressively mark their territory, meaning the barriers to entry would be high.

Instead, Henry and Goldman decided to eyeball companies in the retail sector that needed "industrial financing." These mercantile entities had often relied predominantly on bank loans and commercial paper for funding, but as they sought to expand their business, they needed significant additional capital. This is where Henry Goldman saw a gap and ultimately revolutionized the market – although it was not without its hurdles. One of the challenges for retailers was that, unlike railroads and utilities, these operations had few hard assets—traditionally a key to valuation and underwriting. Henry Goldman advocated a new approach to valuation, not based simply on assets owned but on a company's ability to generate income and, ultimately, its earnings. This earning-based valuation was the key to the firm's first initial public offering and its model for the future when, in 1906, United Cigar Manufacturers, one of the firm's clients, announced to the market that it wanted to expand. The investment bank advised the Cigar group that the best way to raise enough capital to grow was to sell shares to the public. Despite never managing a share offering, Goldman successfully marketed $4.5 million worth of United Cigar shares, and within one year, their stocks were trading on the New York Stock Exchange[55].

A good friend of Henry's – Philip Lehman of Lehman Brothers- shared this new appetite for underwriting. The two would often have lunch together and once even dreamed up a scenario where they would form a new joint company. Though this never materialized, the two investment houses decided to work together to explore new opportunities in underwriting. This was ideal for both as Goldman had a solid customer base, while Lehman Brothers had significant capital at their disposal. They agreed to split the gains from their ventures straight down the middle – 50/50. It was a partnership that would last from their first IPO in 1906 to their last in 1924, including clothing manufacturers, cigar manufacturers, and department stores. On the back of its first-ever initial public offering (IPO), Goldman Sachs co-managed Sears Roebuck (IPO) the same year, raising US$40 million.

Henry Goldman was subsequently invited to join the boards of directors of both United Cigar and Sears. Maintaining a

---

[55] https://www.goldmansachs.com/our-firm/history/moments/1906-united-cigar.html

Goldman partner on the boards of major clients became a tradition at the company. Not long after the Sears deal, Goldman Sachs soon captured larger clients such as May Department Stores, F.W. Woolworth, B.F. Goodrich, H.J. Heinz, Pillsbury, General Foods and Merck. This allowed Goldman Sachs & Co. to offer new products because of its growing clout in the investment market. This, however, came to a halt after the Great Crash of 1929, when its shares fell from $326 to $1.75.

Despite the slowdown in economic activity caused by the Great Depression of the early 1930s, things started to tick up again in 1934 as trading in commercial paper and securities began to rise again. While it continued to expand by taking over other commercial paper firms in New York, Boston, Chicago, and St. Louis, it started to dip into various other investment activities. This included international share offerings (to add to its domestic IPOs), private securities sales, corporate mergers and acquisitions, real estate financing and sales, municipal finance, investment research, block trading, equity and fixed-rate investment portfolios, and options trading. This happened as Congress passed the Securities Act of 1933, which created the Securities and Exchange Commission. This forced Goldman to work diligently to ensure that its investment prospects were more accessible to read and led Goldman Sachs to become very customer-focused. For Goldman, it was all about relationships.

The partnership structure changed slightly during this period as non-family members became partners. One was Sidney J. Weinberg, credited with rescuing the company after the Crash. Born in 1891 in New York, Weinberg joined Goldman in 1907 at 16 as a janitor's assistant.

Notwithstanding such humble beginnings, he soon caught the attention of his bosses for his drive and initiative and was made head of the mailroom. He quickly made an impression on Paul Sachs, so much so that he paid the tuition for Weinberg's first investment banking course at New York University while continuing to guide him toward the higher echelons of the firm. By 1927, he was the second "outsider" to be made partner – becoming senior partner in 1930. At the time of his death in 1969, he was one of the most powerful and iconic figures on Wall Street.

He was nicknamed "Mr. Wall Street" by the New York Times. At one point, holding 35 directorships in companies including Ford, General Electric, Sears, National Dairy Products (now Kraft), and B. F. Goodrich, he was an advisor to five U.S. presidents. Known for his diligence and attention to detail, Weinberg was placed on leave to serve on the government's War Production Board during World War ll. He was called into government service again during the Korean War, serving with the Office of Defense Mobilization. Weinberg was critical to the firm's success and profitability during the 50s and 60s. He was a crucial figure in Ford's IPO in 1956. Having met each other in 1947, the relationship between Henry Ford and Weinberg grew as the years went on. Indeed, it was said that Mr. Wall St. was an informal advisor to the Ford family, and the two would regularly consult over issues relating to Ford Motor Company.

As he looked to restructure the company in a way that would cede some control and voting rights to those outside the immediate Ford family, Weinberg put together a plan that allowed Henry to take Ford public. At $657.9 million and 10.2 million shares, the Ford Motor Company IPO of 1956, led by Goldman Sachs, was the largest joint stock offering to date – making Weinberg one of car manufacturer's first directors from outside the business. The deal was a sea-change on the Street as Ford was considered anti-Semitic.

Following the passing away of Weinberg, Gustave ("Gus") Levy stepped into his shoes as Goldman's Senior partner. Having joined in 1933 from Newborg & Company, he worked his way up from trading foreign bonds to working in its securities arbitrage division alongside Edgar Baruc. His drive and leadership took him up the company's hierarchy – and by the time he took over from Weinberg, Levy was responsible for producing half of the firm's profits due to his block trades and had a ten per cent stake in the firm. (Block trading is when blocks of stocks are bought directly from issuers at an agreed price and then resold to other market participants - at a higher price.)

During his tenure, the firm handled an average of more than 100 million shares annually in trades of 10,000 shares or more on the New York Stock Exchange, according to its website. "When I started out there, Goldman Sachs was probably 5th or 6th place in terms of leading firms, but it wasn't until the late seventies and early eighties when Goldman Sachs - because of its client activity and investment banking, and the deals it did, began to get the reputation for being the gold standard of the investment banking business. A commitment to excellence and a very low tolerance for sloppiness and attention to detail started the talk of a "Goldman culture," which differed from others.

This faded to some degree when the trading era got going," said Roy Smith, a former General Partner at the firm. Speaking on the firm's reputation, Levy said, "We're greedy but long-term greedy, not short-term greedy." [56] John Whitehead said Gus "wanted to do what was right for Goldman Sachs in the long run and didn't deny that he was greedy for that, but he didn't want to be greedy in the short run." Levy's stint came to an unfortunate end as he died from a stroke in 1976. Goldman appointed two senior partners - John L. Weinberg and John Whitehead. The latter, who previously worked out of the firm's I.B. department, noticed that as Goldman gained market share, a growing number of its employees would be new and unfamiliar with its core values. And so, in the late spring of 1979, Whitehead penned a list of principles that defined its core values and, thus, its culture.

He circulated them to his partners and noted: "In earlier eras of the firm's history, these principles could easily be passed along by example and by word of mouth. Now, as we have grown in size and complexity, it seems appropriate to outline

---

[56] https://www.washingtonpost.com/blogs/ezra-klein/post/at-goldman-short-term-greed-vs-long-term-greed/2011/08/25/gIQAxFhhES_blog.html

in writing those policies and principles that have served the firm well over the years and which we expect will guide the actions of all of our people in everything we do in the firm's name[57]."

The principles – which were 14 in all, included the following: 1) Our client's interests come first. 2) Our assets are people, capital, and reputation. 3) We take pride in the professional quality of our work. 4) We stress creativity and imagination in everything we do. 5) We usually try to identify and recruit the best person for every job. 6) We offer our people the opportunity to move ahead more rapidly than is possible in most places. 7) We stress teamwork in everything we do. 8) Our profits are crucial to success. 9) The dedication of our people to the firm and the intensity of their effort to their jobs are greater than one finds in most other organizations. 10) We consider our size an asset. 11) We strive constantly to anticipate the rapidly changing needs of our clients and develop new services to meet their needs. 12) We regularly receive confidential information...to break confidence would be unthinkable. 13) We are fair

---

[57] https://www.goldmansachs.com/our-firm/history/moments/1979-business-principles.html#:~:text=In%20his%20introduction%2C%20Whitehead%20wrote,and%20by%20word%20of%20mouth.

competitors and must never denigrate other firms. 14) Integrity and honesty are at the heart of our business.

To this day, the company continues to abide by these principles. In an interview with the American Prospect, former Goldman VP Wallace Turbeville said employees followed these commandments, "The bankers bought into it. We included these in every presentation and were convinced that clients and potential clients would be persuaded of the firm's trustworthiness given its fine principles. Like the Marines of Weinberg's youth, we were convinced that we were the best of the best." Turbeville conceded that while he and his fellow traders all wanted to make a profit, the temptation for greed was curtailed by these values. "Weinberg forbade participation in hostile takeovers, an immensely lucrative business. When the market crashed in 1987, he refused to take advantage of an "out" in underwriting for the government of Great Britain, knowing that it cost the partners $100 million, and his loss was by far the largest. He blocked every suggestion to take the firm public." But as the leadership changed following Weinberg's departure in the early 1990s – so did the culture. "Our Business Principles" were always featured in the annual report and handed out to new recruits.

But everyone could see that the firm's view of its clients changed. They became a source of transactions, the success of which was measured by the payday, not the enhancement of a long-term relationship. Professional retreats became dominated by speeches about how Goldman had to change to survive," he said. Bob Rubin and Steve Friedman would become co-heads after Weinberg left, with Jon Corzine, Hank Paulson, and Lloyd Blankfein taking the helm one after the other.

During this period, Goldman Sachs would become the envy of Wall Street as one of the allures of working at Goldman was that you could potentially be one of the people running the world. (Rubin served as Secretary of the Treasury under Clinton, Friedman was Assistant to President George W. Bush for Economic Policy and director of the National Economic Council, while Paulson served as Treasury Secretary under Bush.)

Also, "everyone wanted to be like Goldman Sachs or copy it in some ways," according to Roy Smith. Mike Mayo, a Bank Analyst & Managing Director at Wells Fargo Securities, described the old investment bank as going from "caviar to cheeseburgers." For most of its history, Goldman served the most influential people in the world – "heads of states, corporations, millionaires, billionaires," and now it serves regular people worldwide through its various business segments. But despite watching some of its biggest rivals rake in millions of dollars as a result of going public (Bear Sterns in 1985, Morgan Stanley in 1986, and then Lehman Brothers in 1994), Goldman stood pat and retained its partnership structure even though it continued to make big deals like the purchase of the Rockefeller Centre in 1995.

Its former Chairman of Asset Management, Jim O'Neil – who joined in the summer of 95, said that within three months of joining, they had their first considerable debate among all its partners about whether they should or shouldn't go public, and the decision was ultimately that it would not. "For a long time, it was felt that Goldman was unique and it would be better to be private, but over time, frankly, people who were there, though they wouldn't openly say it, got greedy and realized that if they could go public at four times book value, they all stood to make a ton of money and get rich.

There was no real reason at all for Goldman not to go public," said William Cohan.[58] And so it was in May 1999

---

[58] https://www.youtube.com/watch?v=PXgUea6JVcl

that Goldman decided it was time to go public on the New York Stock Exchange – raising $3.7 billion for 69 million shares, making it one of the biggest IPOs at the time. Cohan estimates that the top partners in the region made $300 million each, with less senior partners making about $100 million. After this offering, the firm became officially known as "The Goldman Sachs Group Inc."

This was another sign that things had changed within the firm. Lloyd Blankfein's rise at Goldman Sachs parallels this process. Born in the Bronx, New York City, in 1954, he was the son of a postman who would work night shifts and sort mail in the local post office. His mother worked at a burglar alarm firm – answering calls from prospective clients. Neither of his parents went to college, and the family lived in an apartment in Linden Houses. It was Blankfein, his parents, sister, nephew and grandmother. In his commencement speech in 2013, he tells of his strict upbringing in the Lindon Housing Projects, "It was and is a tough neighbourhood, though it produced some accomplished people who, despite or because of their background, did well."

According to William Cohan, he worked as a lifeguard and served concessions at Yankee Stadium. He attended Thomas

Jefferson High School, where, due to his excellent academics, he was offered the opportunity to graduate a year early (he turned this down). In his last year at school, he became valedictorian (an academic title of success used in the United States, Canada, Philippines, and Armenia, for the student who delivers the closing or farewell statement at a graduation ceremony. [59]The chosen valedictorian is traditionally the student with the highest ranking among their graduating class). This caught the eye of the admission team at Harvard, and they offered him a scholarship, "College was an intimidating place for me. The other students seemed naturally confident; many had travelled and seemed to understand the world.

To this day, I can't forget how insecure I felt, but it made me work harder. Once I realized I belonged, I became more ambitious. Ambition is the inner voice that tells you that you can and should strive to go beyond your circumstances or station in life. You have overcome obstacles, pressures, and self-doubt, and you have done it because you have ambition. You want to succeed for your families and yourselves," he once said. After successfully graduating, he went on to

---

[59] https://www.npr.org/2011/04/11/135246269/goldman-sachs-long-history-of-money-and-power

Harvard Law School – perhaps living out a nickname given to him in grade school. "It kind of always stuck with me," he said, and so had a natural inclination towards becoming a lawyer. "I went to law school and practised for a while. Then, like many people in that era, I wanted to get into finance," he said in an interview with Michael Bloomberg. "I applied to several Wall Street firms, including Goldman Sachs, and got turned down by them, including Goldman Sachs. Which is why, to this day, I admire the firm that I run today," he continued. He finally landed a job at the small commodities trading firm J. Aron & Company in 1981 as a gold bar and coin salesman. Blankfein acknowledged that it wasn't the kind of Wall Street firm he originally intended on joining, "the only job I could get that kind of had, you know, related to Wall Street was J. Aron & Company, which was a commodity trading firm, which on the prestige between equities and fixed income and commodities—commodities was just above a toaster compared to the other jobs," he said.

Luckily for Blankfein, Goldman acquired the commodities brokerage in 1982, so his ticket to the top was set. After showing his bosses his excellent sales acumen, he oversaw six salespeople in the company's foreign exchange trading division. As his influence grew, Lloyd Blankfein came to believe that as the profitability of traditional investment banking started to fade, trading was where it was and played a crucial role in reinventing Goldman Sachs into a profit-creating, risk-taking global financial money manager. The division then took over fixed income and stocks, starting with J. Aron, which had ventured into trading oil and foreign currency.

Blankfein's department now accounted for 80 per cent of Goldman Sachs's profits. "And historically he who controlled the profits controlled the firm," according to Charles D. Ellis, author of The Partnership" – an inside look at Goldman. By 1994, the New Yorker was co-head of trading and three years later became head of Fixed Income, Currency, and Commodities (FICC) – taking advantage of electronic trading technology. In 2004, he was named president and chief operating officer of Goldman Sachs, and two years later, he succeeded Henry Paulson as Chairman and CEO after Paulson was nominated to serve as the secretary of the U.S. Department of the Treasury under President George W. Bush. Blankfein quickly became one of the highest-earning chief executives in Corporate America, accumulating a compensation package of $54 million in 2006 and $70 million the following year.

Despite being named 2009 Person of the Year by the British business newspaper Financial Times. He was also named the "Most Outrageous CEO of 2009 by the American business magazine Forbes – primarily because the CEO had planned to hand out more than $16 billion in year-end bonuses to bankers who – according to the public, had been responsible for the 2008 financial crisis. Blankfein didn't help his cause with comments he made in an interview with the U.K.'s Sunday Times newspaper, where he declared that the bank was "doing God's Work." "We're very important," said Blankfein. "We help companies grow by helping them raise capital. Companies that grow create wealth. This, in turn, allows people to have jobs that create more growth and wealth. It's a virtuous cycle." [60]

The comment drew criticism from all quarters, with CNBC's Rick Ambrose creating a "Lloyds Prayer:[61]

Our Chairman,

Who Art At Goldman,

---

[60] https://www.businessinsider.com/lloyd-blankfein-says-he-is-doing-gods-work-2009-11?r=US&IR=T

[61] https://www.cnbc.com/2009/11/10/the-lloyds-prayer.html

Blankfein Be Thy Name.

The Rally's Come.

God's Work Be Done,

We Have No Fear Of Correction.

Give Us This Day Our Daily Gains,

And Bankrupt Our Nearest Competitors,

Just As You Taught Lehman And Bear A Lesson.

And Bring Us Not Under Indictment.

For Thine Is The Treasury,

The House And The Senate

Forever And Ever.

Goldman.

In an interview with Charlie Rose, Blankfein understood why he and his fellow CEOs were public enemy number one: "The financial system failed the American people... "How could you not blame the people [on Wall Street] that had awfully nice lives while things were going well? How could you not blame them when things turned badly?" [62]

But was Blankfein right? Were he and his fellow bankers really doing "God's Work?" One could look at the Parable of the Talents in Matthew 25 and argue that what Goldman and the rest of Wall Street were doing perfectly aligned with scripture. Subtitled "The Story of Investment" by Eugene Patterson in the Message Bible translation, the parable tells the story of a Master who went on an extended trip.

Still, before he went, he delegated responsibilities to his three servants, "To one he gave five thousand dollars, to another two thousand, to a third one thousand, depending on their abilities. Then he left. The first servant immediately went to work and doubled his master's investment. The second did the same. But the man with the single thousand dug a hole and carefully buried his master's money." After a long absence, the master of those three servants returned and settled up with them. "The one given five thousand dollars showed him how he had doubled his investment. His master commended him: 'Good work! You did your job well. From now on, be my partner.' Sounds familiar?

---

[62] https://www.youtube.com/watch?v=g4XudhBQRy8

The second servant with the two thousand showed how he had doubled his master's investment. He was also commended, 'Good work! You did your job well. From now on, be my partner.' However, when the third servant told his master that he had dug his money into the ground, he was furious, 'The least you could have done would have been to invest the sum with the bankers, where at least I would have gotten a little interest. Take the thousand and give it to the one who risked the most. And get rid of this "play-it-safe" who won't go out on a limb. Throw him out."

Seen from this perspective, the investment and trading principles of the master and his servants would be in line with regular Wall Street activity: take your client's money and flip it for even more cash than the original investment - Economics 101. And so, on the surface, Blankfein and Co. were doing everything correctly. Furthermore, if you look at the parable of the sower – you see once more that God is interested in multiplication. In this parable, Jesus tells of the story of a farmer who sowed seed - and as he sowed, some seed fell by the wayside; some fell on stony places, some fell among thorns, but others fell on good ground. Of those that fell on the wayside - the birds came and devoured them. Those that fell on stony places did not have much earth; they immediately sprang up because they had no depth of land, but when the sun was up, they were scorched, and because they had no root, they withered away. And some fell among thorns, and the thorns sprang up and choked them. But that seed that fell on good ground bore fruit and produced: "some a hundredfold, some sixty, some thirty."

So, to put it into financial terms, seed can represent investment – and the investment sowed into a good investment scheme reaped 30 times, 60 times, or 100 times as much as what was initially invested. Therefore, God is very much interested in sowing (or investing) and gaining a harvest. But it's important to note that the Bible says, "whether you eat or drink, or whatever you do, do all to the glory of God." (1 Corinthians 10:31).

In other words – while God has nothing against investing and trading for multiple gains – he wants us to do it in a manner that glorifies him. Moreover, the Book of Proverbs says, "Better is a little with righteousness than great revenues with injustice." (Proverbs 16:8). Therefore, producing a lower return on investment in a righteous manner is better than high-flying profits unjustly. And this is where Blankfein's idea that they were doing God's work falls down.

In April 2010, Goldman Sachs' officials were accused of "defrauding" investors by misstating and omitting key facts about a financial product tied to subprime mortgages. Goldman was quick to refute the allegations as "completely unfounded." One Goldman email – sent days after being accused – to the office of the head of the European Commission said: "Goldman Sachs would never condone one of its employees misleading anyone, certainly not investors counterparties or clients." [63]But by July 2010, the bank had settled with the U.S. authorities by paying a $550 million fine, the most significant penalty imposed on a Wall Street bank. In settlement papers submitted to the U.S. District Court for the Southern District of New York, Goldman made the following acknowledgement:

"Goldman acknowledges that the marketing materials for the ABACUS 2007-AC1 transaction contained incomplete information. In particular, it was a mistake for the Goldman marketing materials to state that the reference portfolio was "selected by" ACA Management LLC without disclosing the role of Paulson & Co. Inc. in the portfolio selection process and that Paulson's economic interests were adverse to CDO

---

[63] https://www.cbsnews.com/news/why-5-billion-goldman-sachs-settlement-is-a-slap-on-the-tentacle/

investors. Goldman regrets that the marketing materials did not contain that disclosure." [64]

Said Robert Khuzami, Director of the SEC's Division of Enforcement. "This settlement is a stark lesson to Wall Street firms that no product is too complex, and no investor too sophisticated, to avoid a heavy price if a firm violates the fundamental principles of honest treatment and fair dealing." Khuzami's statement violates Goldman's principles – particularly its 14th one, which states, "Integrity and honesty are at the heart of our business." [65] A few years ago, Goldman Sachs Group Inc. agreed to pay $20 million to settle an investor lawsuit accusing bank traders, and 15 other financial institutions of rigging prices for bonds Fannie Mae and Freddie Mac issued. This once more goes against honest trading and is unjust – and therefore unbiblical because scripture says, "Guard my common good: Do what's right and do it in the right way" (Is 56:1). This is not the only time the Bible talks about justice. "This is what the Lord says: Do what is just and right" (Jeremiah 22:3). "Follow justice and

---

[64] https://www.sec.gov/litigation/litreleases/lr-21592#:~:text=Goldman%20acknowledges%20that%20the%20marketing,Inc.

[65] https://www.csmonitor.com/Business/2010/0715/Goldman-Sachs-550-million-settlement-a-stark-lesson-for-Wall-Street

justice alone" (Deuteronomy 16:20). "For the LORD is righteous, he loves justice." (Psalm 11:7).

As it enters into a new decade (and now under new leadership with David M. Solomon taking over Blankfein in 2019), Goldman is trying to change its image and regain favour with Wall Street by opening its doors to shareholders, analysts, the media, and even regulators for its first "investor day." This marks a significant shift from the bank's historic secrecy. "We are taking real and significant steps to make Goldman Sachs more transparent and easier to understand," Solomon said in a statement[66].

So perhaps under Solomon, Goldman will find a better way of doing God's Work than Mr. Blankfein...

---

[66] https://www.goldmansachs.com/media-relations/press-releases/current/announcement-01-29-2020.html

"Anyone who says money doesn't buy happiness just doesn't know where to go for shopping."

"Money won't make you happy, but it's nicer to cry in a Ferrari."

Happy Money

I WAS TWENTY-SEVEN years old and on the verge of becoming a multimillionaire. I'd made it. I'd achieved. My life looked exactly like I'd wanted it to look. And with a sinking feeling of horror, a question that had been sitting on the periphery of my conscience stepped forward into the light. So why am I so miserable? [67]That was the stark conclusion that former Wall Street trader Sam Polk came to in his memoir/part exposé of the money-obsessed culture on The Street. Indeed, in *For the Love of Money*, Polk chronicles the story of an individual who eventually channelled his initiable desire for money into becoming a transformative philanthropist.

Born in Southern California to a devoted mother and a blundering and dismissive father, Polk could only dream of a day when money was not an option and he wouldn't have

---

[67] https://www.amazon.co.uk/Love-Money-Memoir-Sam-Polk/dp/1476785988

to live paycheck to paycheck as his family did. (He noted in an interview with CNBC that his dad always talked about making it big and what life would be like if they were rich). In his memoir, Sam recounts his days as a young kid at summer camp, where he would routinely get bullied because of his weight, and how once he reached High School, he transformed into a competitive student – coming out top in both grades and also sports – even coming out ahead of his twin brother, Ben, who had been the one protecting him from bullies in their summer camp days. Accepted by Columbia University, he caught his first break on Wall Street by successfully navigating his way into a summer internship at the former Swiss banking giant Credit Suisse First Boston – working on a frantic stock market trading floor just as he had so fondly read in Michael Lewis's Liar's Poker. Interestingly, despite not necessarily being "happy" during his early days on the street, he describes how he loved the "intellectual challenge of analyzing bonds and companies, the fact that you had to read the news and understand world events because they impact your trades. I loved it. I wanted to be the guys I saw daily who had made it. Not only did they have these awesome positions of authority, but you could tell by listening to them talk that they made more money than anyone I'd ever known." [68]

Thrilled to receive a $40,000 bonus working at Bank of America, the seeds of envy sprouted when he heard that a fellow trader who only had a few years on him in terms of experience was snagged by Credit Suisse F.B. for $900,000. However, he turned this envy into ambition. He turned his thoughts into how much he could make by working tirelessly up the Wall Street ladder – becoming a bond and credit default swap trader earning north of $1.5 million. Yet, as he candidly described it in his famous NYTimes Op-ed, earning $1 million or $2 million didn't look so "sweet" when the managing director sitting next to you makes more than $10 million yearly. Polk now wanted to be rich like his bosses and a billionaire who could rub shoulders with the same mayors and senators who go to court-side games featuring the Lakers and the Knicks, which his colleagues did.

This undefeated drive to be rich culminated after a near-decade on Wall Street when he was offered a bonus of $3.6 million — and was angry because it wasn't big enough. And

---

[68] https://www.cnbc.com/2016/08/05/how-i-left-wall-street-and-launched-a-start-upcommentary.html

it was at that moment he realized that he had developed an addiction. He did not have an addiction to the drugs and alcohol that nearly got him kicked out of college. But a person with an addiction to wealth. It was almost like, according to Polk, "in the months before bonuses were handed out, the trading floor started to feel like a neighbourhood in The Wire when the heroin runs out." [69]

There's no doubt that Polk's story resonates not just throughout The Street but also across the biggest financial centres across the world, like London, Tokyo, and San Francisco. Indeed, at just 27 years old, young multimillionaire Duncan Riach went further than saying that money doesn't make us happy – it doesn't make you content, either. Having worked at a Silicon Valley technology company that designs and markets cutting-edge computer processing chips, Duncan was making north of $500,000 a year, yet told CNBC that "it's really challenging being wealthy. Approach with caution." He learned first-hand that money can't buy happiness - in fact, money can make life worse because it can distract us from our deeper issues by spending money on things we don't need or worrying about

---

[69] https://www.nytimes.com/2014/01/19/opinion/sunday/for-the-love-of-money.html

losing our wealth. "Life might also get much more complicated with wealth," he said. And so he said the trick was figuring out how much money you need to live a reasonable lifestyle. Duncan measures true wealth by your discipline to live frugally, your choice to invest rather than spend, and your ability to live longer without working. Polk's admission that the money, power, and prestige he had on Wall Street failed to fill the empty void he had on the inside presents an age-old question: Can money really buy us happiness? It's a question that many economists, psychologists, and philosophers have grappled with for centuries, with every passing week seemingly producing new research that either argues for or against the argument that money can bring us happiness.

Indeed, a 2023 research paper by Nobel-Prize-winning economist Daniel Kahneman and fellow psychologist Matthew Killingsworth [70] found that for most people, happiness does improve with higher earnings — but only up to a point. (That point being a cool $500,000 a year). "In the simplest terms, this suggests that for most people, larger incomes are associated with greater happiness,"

---

[70] https://www.pnas.org/doi/10.1073/pnas.2208661120

Killingsworth said. The exception is people who are financially well-off but unhappy. For instance, if you're rich and miserable, more money won't help."

However, the pair and their fellow researchers found a small sample for which earning higher incomes made little difference. The relationship between happiness and income differs for this "unhappy group," comprising roughly 15% of the sample data. Their "unhappiness diminishes with rising income up to a threshold, then shows no further progress." These people tend to experience negative "miseries" that typically cannot be alleviated by earning more money through things such as a break-up, bereavement of a spouse, or clinical depression.

One of the main reasons why having more money doesn't always make us happy is that we adapt to it. "Human beings are remarkably good at getting used to changes in their lives, especially positive changes," said Sonja Lyubomirsky, a psychology professor at the University of California, Riverside, in an interview with The New York Times. "If you have a rise in income, it gives you a boost, but then your aspirations rise too. Maybe you buy a bigger home in a new neighbourhood, so your neighbours are richer, and you start wanting even more. You've stepped on the hedonic treadmill. Trying to prevent that or slow it down is a challenge." [71] Economist Richard Easterlin identified this phenomenon in the 1970s in what's now known as the Easterlin Paradox. In his paper titled, "Does Economic Growth Improve the Human Lot? Easterlin asks, "Would giving everyone more money make everyone happier?" [72]

From the perspective of an economist, if you gave people more money (throw it out of a helicopter, as some economists like to put it), they would be able to buy more goods and services over some time, leading to greater economic growth as measured by Real Gross Domestic Product. Indeed, with this extra liquidity, households can buy the latest iPhone or the newest Tesla, go to a five-star gym, etc. All of which should make them better off than before they received this extra cash in every single way. In other words, this should make them happier.

---

[71] https://www.nytimes.com/2019/03/29/smarter-living/what-to-do-when-youre-bored-with-your-routines.html#:~:text=%E2%80%9CHumans%20are%20remarkably%20good%20at,Riverside%2C%20who%20studies%20hedonic%20adaptation.

[72] https://www.sciencedirect.com/science/article/abs/pii/B9780122050503500087

However, is this actual reality? To determine whether this was true, he first had to define what he meant by "happiness." According to Easterlin, happiness is "life satisfaction." This is simply asking someone on a scale of 0-10 how satisfied they are with their life. He then used this definition to ask two key questions. The first was, are more affluent people happier than poorer people in the same country? The second question was, if everyone in a country becomes more prosperous over time, do they all become happier? If we look at Easterlin's first question and if we were to focus on relative incomes as opposed to average incomes in a country where, for example, average incomes are around $25,000, if someone earns $39,000, they would be considered relatively rich in this country. And someone who makes $11,000 would be regarded as relatively poor in this country compared to the average person.

Therefore, as one would expect, more affluent people were, in fact, happier than poorer people in the same country. However, this was different from the question he was particularly interested in. He was more intrigued to know whether if everyone in a country becomes more prosperous over time, they all also become happier. The best example is Japan, where the average income increased fivefold from 1958 to 1987. To put this into layperson's terms, if in 1958 only 1% of households in Japan owned a car, by 1987, 60% of households owned a car.

The change was so significant that he split the country by income into three groups in 1958, and by 1987, he found that the people in the lowest group would have been making more money than those in the highest group in 1958. And so, from his research, increasing everyone's income over time does not affect their happiness. People were just as happy (or sad) as before. This wasn't only in Japan but also across all the other countries still studied, including the US. But why is this the case? If everyone in society becomes more affluent, people's perceptions of luxury and what it means to live a good life change with them, meaning that you now need much more than you did before to feel comfortable. It's a race you can never really win.

According to Duncan Riach, if one equates their worth to how much they have in their bank account, they will always notice those who have more than themselves and will always feel that they don't "measure up." He said that if you suffer from this, you won't get to some "magical level" of net worth and finally realize that you are worth more. The problem is going to get worse.

Many studies show that people's ideas of a good income increase as they earn more. People in wealthier countries have very different standards of a comfortable life compared to people in relatively poorer countries, so everyone becomes wealthier. According to this new normative definition, what they used to think of as a comfortable life is no longer valid, meaning they're still not living a comfortable, happy life. Ultimately, income can only affect happiness if you become wealthier than your counterparts. At the same time, if everyone else stays the same or becomes poorer, you'll be happier about it, or if everyone else becomes poorer. At the same time, you remain the same, and you'll still be happier for it, but if everyone becomes the richest together, it makes no difference.

American political scientist and political psychologist Robert Edwards Lane says in his book, The Loss of Happiness in Market Democracies, "Amidst the satisfaction people feel with their material progress, there is a spirit of unhappiness and depression haunting advanced market democracies throughout the world." So former hip-hip star Christopher Wallace, better known as the Notorious B.I.G or "Biggie," may have been right when he said, "Mo' money… Mo' problems."

To be sure, he wasn't the only wealthy public figure to espouse the same issues with money:

Consider the quotes from the following:

John D. Rockefeller: "I have made many millions, but they have brought me no happiness."

W.H. Vanderbilt: "The care of $200 million is enough to kill anyone. There is no pleasure in it."

John Jacob Astor: "I am the most miserable man on earth."

Henry Ford: "I was happier doing a mechanic's job."

Andrew Carnegie: "Millionaires seldom smile."

It's easy to see why affluence would lead to dissatisfaction. Whatever we have, we wish that we had more. It goes back to basic Economics 101, where we have unlimited wants but limited ability to meet those wants. Even the writer of Ecclesiastes says those who love money will never have enough. "How meaningless to think wealth brings true happiness!" he says. (Ecclesiastes 5:10)

So where can we find this happiness that seems so elusive for most of us? The first thing you'll notice is that most people try to find joy in material items, sometimes in landing the "perfect" job, or better still, finding happiness in another person. The only problem is that these material things are temporary. You might buy the latest Range Rover or iPhone – only for the same company to release a newer version the following year. Furthermore, perhaps you've been promoted to a managing director – only to discover a higher-ranking job elsewhere.

Or, after a few years of marriage, you find out that your partner can never truly make you happy because all of us, as human as we are, are flawed in our little ways. There is a person, though, that can satisfy the longing soul and fill the hungry soul when the world can't. And the best news is that, fortunately, we don't need to look far for that person. The Psalmist says, "Delight yourself in the LORD, and he will give you the desires of your heart." (Psalm 37:4). The word "Delight" here means finding joy, pleasure, and satisfaction in something or someone. And so, in this context, it refers to seeing these things in the Lord and not in earthly wealth.

Moreover, for this to happen, one has to delight oneself in the Lord by developing a deep and intimate relationship with Him, seeking His presence, and experiencing the joy and fulfilment that come from knowing Him. It's not surprising then that the Psalmist says about the lord, "You make known to me the path of life; in your presence, there is fullness of joy; at your right hand are pleasures forevermore." Here, the Psalmist recognizes that true joy and happiness are found in the presence of God, and it is in Him that we experience abundant and eternal pleasures – not the fleeting ones associated with numbers on a piece of paper.

This is the first starting point if you seek true happiness away from what the world offers. This part of the verse implies that we have to prioritize the LORD above all else, making Him the centre of our life and finding true contentment in Him rather than in material possessions. Hence, in Matthew 6:33, Jesus tells his followers to "seek first the kingdom of God and his righteousness, and all these things will be added to you." In other words, when we prioritize our relationship with God and seek His ways, He will provide for our needs - financial and otherwise. It implies prioritizing God above all else, making Him the centre of one's life, and finding true contentment in Him rather than worldly pursuits or possessions. According to the Psalmist, only then will He give you the desires of your heart. "Desires" refers to our hearts' longings, aspirations, and wishes.

When we delight in the Lord, our desires align with His will. This is the most important part because, as noted earlier,

God's will is certainly not for us to love money (1 Timothy 6:10). Therefore, our hearts become transformed, and we begin to desire the things that are pleasing to God and not pleasing to our narrow perception of what happiness is. However, this doesn't mean that every desire we have will be granted, as some desires may be opposite to God's will or not in our best interest. Instead, it means God will fulfil our hearts' true and righteous desires.

And so you might be asking, what practical steps can you take to find happiness in God? Chief among them is this: Seeking God wholeheartedly with everything you have. Jeremiah 29:13 says, "You will seek me and find me when you seek me with all your heart." This means making a conscious decision to pursue a genuine and intimate relationship with God. This will involve setting aside time for prayer, studying His Word (the Bible), and seeking to know Him more deeply. To supplement this, one has to Meditate on God's Word: Set aside regular time to read and reflect on Scripture. Psalm 1:2 says, "But his delight is in the law of the LORD, and on his law, he meditates day and night."

Unless we allow God's Word to shape our thoughts and beliefs, we will be stuck with the mindset of the culture we're living in – which, of course, involves chasing that extra dollar or two. Ultimately, it will involve doing something counter-cultural and not something that is done often in this day and age: Developing an attitude of gratitude.

The Book of Thessalonians advises us to "give thanks in all circumstances." Develop a habit of gratitude by intentionally focusing on the blessings and goodness of God in your life. That could be giving thanks for the job you have, your spouse, your children, etc. So perhaps keep a gratitude journal and express thankfulness to God regularly. Gratitude helps shift our perspective and cultivates happiness.

Remember, finding happiness in God is an ongoing journey that requires consistent effort and a sincere heart. As you seek Him and align your life with His principles, you will discover a deep and abiding joy that surpasses temporary circumstances and fills your life with meaning and purpose.

"When you set your eyes on wealth, it is [suddenly] gone. For wealth certainly makes itself wings Like an eagle that flies to the heavens." - Proverbs 23:5

A Salary of Smoke

IMAGINE YOU ARE about to celebrate your 15th wedding anniversary with your wife and looking for fresh flowers to surprise her on the morning of your special day. So you come across a bouquet of tulips sitting on the windowsill of your local grocery store. How much would you pay for them - a few pounds? Maybe a hundred pounds because it's a special occasion? How about a million? No chance, right?

How much would you pay for a fancy house in the centre of London or be part owner of a website that sells gardening products? At various points in our history, tulips, property, and shares in Garden.com have all sold for much more than they were worth. In each case, the price rose and rose and then suddenly crashed. These are known as bubbles. It was once said that Benjamin Franklin, one of the leading figures of early American history, said there were only two things certain in life: death and taxes. However, this author would like to add a third certainty, which economists call the "economic cycle." And it's within the economic cycle where we can experience such bubbles. So, what exactly goes on with a bubble? Let's go back to our tulips story earlier to get a better idea.

Called "Tulip Mania," the early 17th century saw the Netherlands enter a golden age of economic prosperity as the Port of Amsterdam became Europe's most influential commercial port and town (think the city of London or Wall Street in today's parlance). The port became popular as Dutch ships imported spices from Asia in considerable quantities to earn profits in Europe. As a result, the country experienced a surge in wealth, which enabled the merchants and traders who worked at the ports to buy large properties – including mansions

surrounded by beautiful flower gardens. But there was one flower in exceptionally high demand: the tulip. Seen a luxury item because of its rarity and because they took a long time to grow – they were all the rage in the Netherlands by the mid-1630s. However, because these particular tulips were so rare and grew so much in popularity, more and more buyers drove up the prices of tulips. At one point, a single tulip bulb sold for more than ten times the annual salary of a typical worker. Indeed, by some accounts, the price for a rare type of tulip bulb was equivalent to $50,000. [73]

Thus, a bubble was born. The term "bubble," in the financial context, generally refers to a situation where the price for an asset exceeds its fundamental or intrinsic value by a large margin, as seen with the tulips example.

These assets may include an individual stock, a financial asset, a sector of a market (think the tech sector during the dot-com bubble), or many others. Generally, bubbles fall under four different categories[74]: stock market bubbles (equities), asset market bubbles (other industries or sections of the economy other than the equities market), credit bubbles (a sudden increase in loans), commodity bubbles (an increase in commodity prices like tulips).

Moreover, in his 1986 book, Stabilizing an Unstable Economy, economist Hyman P. Minsky identified the five stages of a bubble, starting with the first: Displacement. In this instance, investors begin to get very bullish or excited about a new or innovative product or technology, and for good reason in most cases. The second stage is what's

---

[73] https://www.jstor.org/stable/1830454
[74] https://www.thestreet.com/dictionary/b/bubble

known as the boom phase, in which the price of the asset or commodity steadily begins to climb and then instantly skyrockets upward, attracting media hype along with new investors.

The third is called euphoria, a blissful stage in which prices continue to climb, and people are swept up believing that no matter how high the prices get, someone will always be willing to buy. People think that whatever price they buy their asset at, they can't lose because when they eventually come to sell it off, it will go for much more than what they purchased it for. But at this stage, sensible investors begin to clock onto the fact that the actual value of a product, like a tulip, isn't in line with what they paid, so they cash out. This leads us to the profit-taking phase, which is the fourth stage. Here, some people predict that the bubble is about to burst – a tricky prediction to make with accuracy – and begin to sell. The fifth and final stage is panic. Relatively self-explanatory, this stage consists of sharply declining prices and panicking investors selling as quickly as possible to recoup their losses, ultimately causing a bubble to burst.

We recently saw this kind of panic during the dot-com bubble, which began in the early to mid-1990s. It was an era of technological advancement that accelerated in 1993 with the release of the Mosaic web browser, which meant that many people could access the Internet for the first time. At the same time, slow personal computers – which were once a luxury- have now become an essential household fixture.

This new mass adoption brought a gold rush of opportunity, which led to the creation of a wave of Internet companies. One of these companies, Netscape, decided to distribute its web browser freely, and it quickly became the industry standard. Within a year, the Netscape browser's popularity prompted the company to go public on the stock market.

On August 9, 1995, Netscape's initial public offering took the world by storm when their opening stock price of $28 soared to $75 on their first day of trading. [75]It was unusual for a company to go public before being profitable. The success of Netscape's IPO sent shockwaves around the world. Many people who had just begun using the internet saw the success of Netscape and wanted to capitalize on the growing opportunity.

With a decline in interest rates and a new act lowering capital gains taxes in the US, investors now had more capital and

---

[75] https://www.poynter.org/reporting-editing/2015/the-netscape-moment-20-years-on/

became more willing to make speculative investments. This initial displacement is standard in any bubble and occurs when something new catches investors' attention. Whether it be a new product, technology, or economic policy, a change in the system sets the stage for a bubble to form.

However, as market participants, we shouldn't always believe the hype. As time passed, more and more investors rushed to fund new internet companies as they watched the success of those that went public.

Many companies that had barely generated profits began launching initial public offerings on the Nasdaq Stock Exchange. Instead of focusing on profit maximization, many of these companies were focused on spending massive amounts of money on advertising to build their market share as fast as possible. This meant many were highly unprofitable, but this appeared not to matter. In 1999, there were 457 IPOs, [76] most of which doubled in price on their first day of trading. As euphoria continued to hit investors because the price of technology stocks skyrocketed, caution

---

[76] https://www.wired.com/insights/2013/08/tech-boom-2-0-lessons-learned-from-the-dot-com-crash/#:~:text=In%201999%2C%20there%20were%20457,%2C%20WorldCom%20and%20FreeInternet.com.

was thrown to the wind. There was news of price increases spurring investor enthusiasm, and word-of-mouth excitement caused further price increases, a positive feedback loop with increasing stock prices. It reinforced people's initial decision to buy more stock compared to the second stage of a bubble investor.

The confidence level reaches an all-time high as prices in the market begin to explode, with more and more people looking to cash in on the emerging opportunity. The trouble is some of the hype is genuine, but which bit to believe?

Despite doubts about the underlying value of these investments, many began to be drawn to them mainly through a fear of missing out; you could call it a stock market firm or extreme investor enthusiasm that continued to drive prices up to levels not supported by fundamentals and instead, rested on psychological factors, irrational exuberance, and overconfidence, figuring out when the bubble will enter its final stage and burst is challenging.

Noticing the warning signs can be especially difficult given the growing enthusiasm people share as the prices continue to rise. The best way is to dig deeper and see whether fundamentals support these decisions or are indeed just irrational exuberance. As the bubble expanded rapidly, things would soon change with the year turning to 2000 and the y2k computer bug no longer a worry; the US Federal Reserve announced plans to raise interest rates aggressively. This led to significant stock market volatility as analysts disagreed on whether or not technology companies would be affected by higher borrowing costs.

On March 10, the Nasdaq reached an all-time high of more than 5,000 points - a five-fold increase in five years. However, just three days later, news broke that Japan had again entered a recession[77]. When a global event such as that significantly damages investor confidence, many people start panic selling with no more investors willing to buy at elevated prices and a massive sell-off underway. The bubble had burst.

Once a bubble has burst, it will not inflate again. The panic that follows a bubble can be devastating. Often, this fear and uncertainty can spread to other asset classes and can even cause a recession. Technology stocks began losing value faster than they had gained it. By the fall of 2000, most internet stocks had declined by 75%, wiping out $1.75

---

[77] https://www.wired.com/2010/03/0310nasdaq-bust/

trillion in value. Most dot-com companies that once had multi-million dollar valuations began to default.

So, what could we take away from all this? When it comes to new technologies, people are eager to take advantage of the next big thing. The greatly respected investor Warren Buffett famously stayed out of all this. His reasoning was simply that the internet industry wasn't within his area of expertise, and because of this, he wasn't going to buy those types of stocks. Unlike most other investors, he didn't buy into the hype despite the world going mad for internet stocks.

There's nothing new about bubbles as history finds a way of repeating itself, and for as long as new stories that inspire mass enthusiasm for new types of investment continue to emerge, we will see more of them – and sure enough, we did.

***

In the early 2000s, the Federal Reserve – the central bank in the U.S. lowered interest rates to stimulate economic growth and prevent a recession after the dot-com bubble burst. Specifically, the Fed lowered the federal funds rate, the interest rate at which banks lend and borrow from each other overnight, from 6.5% in May 2000 to 1% in June 2003 –

taking them to their lowest level since 1958 at the time[78]. Indeed, it decreased rates thirteen times since the beginning of 2001. These low-interest rates made borrowing cheaper and more accessible, encouraging people to take out mortgages. As a result, mortgage lenders began offering mortgages to borrowers with either low creditworthiness or altogether lousy credit. These are called subprime borrowers. These mortgages often had adjustable interest rates, which could increase over time. Once a large number of these loans were issued, banks and financial institutions pooled these loans together to reduce the risks associated with subprime mortgages.

This process is known as securitization. This mortgage pool is used as collateral to create mortgage-backed securities (MBS). To make things even more complicated, these MBS were further divided into different tranches with varying levels of risk and sold to investors. At the same time, the low interest rates led to a boom in the U.S. housing market, driving up housing prices nationwide. Adjusting for inflation, real U.S. house prices rose 34% during 2000-

---

[78] https://www.latimes.com/archives/la-xpm-2000-mar-13-nc-8458-story.html

2005[79]. Specific regions experienced even faster appreciation; in 2004 alone, housing in Miami, Los Angeles, and West Palm Beach appreciated more than 20%, and Las Vegas appreciated 35%.

The surge in the housing market caught the eye of investors looking for quick profits. Subsequently, these investors started snapping up multiple properties to flip them at a higher price later. This, of course, further fuelled house prices. However, these prices became detached from the underlying value of the properties, much like the internet stocks during the Dotcom bubble - resulting in an overvaluation of the housing market.

This overvaluation created a housing bubble. Eventually, housing prices reached a point where they were no longer sustainable. Central to this were the adjustable-rate mortgages with low introductory interest rates, which were later adjusted to higher rates.

As these rates began to rise, many subprime homeowners could not afford to make their monthly payments, leading to widespread defaults. Unsurprisingly, the value of the

---

[79] https://www.federalreserve.gov/newsevents/speech/bernanke20100103a.htm

Mortgage-backed Securities plummeted, leading to significant losses for investors. And these weren't any old investors. These were some of the biggest financial institutions in the world with a wealth of history behind them, such as Goldman Sachs, JP Morgan, and Lehman Brothers, to name a few.

These banks were left holding trillions of dollars worth of near-worthless investments in subprime mortgages and other complex financial assets/securities on their balance sheets. This led to widespread panic from New York to Hong Kong and everywhere in between, as alarm bells started ringing about the safety of the global financial system.

The first domino to tilt was Bear Stearns, one of the largest investment banks on Wall Street, with the collapse of its hedge funds in late 2006 that invested heavily in mortgage-backed securities tied to subprime mortgages. This triggered a run on the bank, and by March 13, 2008, Bear Stearns only had $2 billion left in cash[80]. In the end, the US Federal Reserve facilitated a bailout of Bear Stearns by arranging for rival investment bank JPMorgan Chase to acquire it for $2 a

---

[80] https://www.researchgate.net/figure/Appreciation-of-House-Prices-1996-2007-percentage-change-year-by-year_fig3_262663118

share - a steep decline from the $170 share price that Bear stock had fetched just a year earlier[81].

The bailout of Bear only provided a respite for the financial system as by September 15, 2008, Lehman Brothers, a major investment bank heavily involved in subprime mortgages, filed for bankruptcy, marking the largest bankruptcy filing in U.S. history. This, alongside the bailout of insurance giant AIG, sent the US stock market into a tailspin a week later, with the Dow Jones Industrial Average falling by 777.68 points, the largest single-day point loss.

And it didn't stop there – on October 13, 2008, The Dow Jones experienced another significant decline, dropping 936.42 points, representing a decline of 7.87%. All in all, the global financial crisis of 2008, when looked at from the perspective of the United States, led to 8.8 million job losses, 8 million home foreclosures, $7.4 trillion in stock wealth lost from 2008-09 ($66,200 per household on average), evaporation of $19.2 trillion in household wealth, and a 40%

---

[81] https://www.history.com/this-day-in-history/bear-stearns-sold-to-j-p-morgan-chase

decline in house prices[82]. The global pandemic due to COVID-19 also caused similar falls in wealth.

For example, in the United States, the S&P 500, a widely used benchmark for U.S. stocks, experienced a rapid decline of around 34% from its peak in February 2020 to its lowest in March 2020. European stock markets also saw significant declines[83]. The Euro Stoxx 50, which tracks the performance of Eurozone blue-chip stocks, fell by about 40% from its peak in February to its low in March. Furthermore, Asian stock markets were also heavily impacted. The MSCI Asia Pacific Index, which includes stocks from various countries in the Asia-Pacific region, experienced a drop of around 30% during the same period[84].

All in all, stock markets in other regions, including emerging markets, also experienced sharp declines as the pandemic's economic impact spread worldwide. The global financial crisis and the "COVID Crash" following the recent global pandemic serve as a great reminder of the following Proverb

---

[82] https://www.sec.gov/Archives/edgar/data/19617/000089882208000286/pressrelease.htm
[83] https://www.bls.gov/opub/mlr/2011/04/art1full.pdf
[84] https://www.cnbc.com/2021/03/16/one-year-ago-stocks-dropped-12percent-in-a-single-day-what-investors-have-learned-since-then.html

in the Old Testament Bible, which states: "Cast but a glance at riches, and they are gone, for they will surely sprout wings and fly off to the sky like an eagle." (Proverbs 23:5).

This verse offers a cautionary tale about the temporary nature of wealth and the potential dangers of pursuing it excessively or placing too much importance on material possessions. The words "cast but a glance" (used by the writer of the King James version of the Bible) suggest a fleeting or passing look, indicating that we as individuals.

One should focus on something other than wealth. It indicates that merely glancing at riches can lead to their disappearance or loss circa the dotcom crash and the 2008 crisis, as outlined above. The writer isn't saying here that we are to ignore riches – we should acknowledge it but not fixate our hearts and eyes on them – meaning that we need to maintain a balanced perspective and not allow the pursuit of wealth to become a stranglehold on our lives.

Delving deeper into the issue, the writer uses a strong metaphor to re-emphasize his point: "For they will surely sprout wings and fly off to the sky like an eagle." Just as an eagle swiftly takes flight and soars high in the sky, wealth can vanish unexpectedly and be beyond one's reach. The comparison highlights the suddenness and unpredictability of wealth's departure, reinforcing that it should not be the sole focus or source of one's security and happiness. As a matter of fact, by acknowledging the transient nature of money, we can set realistic expectations about what can happen to money.

Therefore, we gain a new perspective on our relationship with it. This point was reinforced later on in the book of Proverbs when the writer points out to the reader that "A man's strength, power, and riches will one day fade away; not even nations endure forever" (Proverbs 27:24).

It implies that even the most powerful leaders or nations will only maintain their position temporarily. Power dynamics shift, political systems change, and new leaders emerge. As history has shown, no empire or ruling dynasty remains in control forever. Therefore, to think that the same cannot happen to something as material as wealth and riches would be a massive misjudgment. Suppose it's not economic fluctuations (e.g., the financial crisis or dotcom bubble). In that case, the mismanagement of money, natural disasters, or simply the passage of time (think inflation) – worldly possessions can never be eternal.

Perhaps this is why the Apostle Paul, the writer of the Book of Timothy, stresses to his audience the need to "Command those who are rich in this present world not to be arrogant nor to put their hope in wealth, which is so uncertain, but to put their hope in God, who richly provides us with everything for our enjoyment" (Timothy 6:17). This verse forms part of a larger letter in which he advises a young church leader named Timothy, on several matters, including the appropriate attitude towards wealth. He underscores again that money is not a stable or reliable foundation to base one's hope and security.

Instead, Paul urges the rich to anchor their hope in God. He does so because, ultimately, God is the only provider and sustainer of all things. He generously provides all that is needed for enjoyment and fulfilment in life. This includes material possessions and valuable items such as health, relationships, and spiritual well-being – all things wealth cannot buy.

[13] https://www.statista.com/topics/6311/coronavirus-covid-19-in-asia-pacific/

"The lesson is clear. Inflation devalues us all."

- Margaret Thatcher.

The Cost of Living: A Monetary Phenomenon

IN THE PREVIOUS chapter, we saw how it only takes one boom to go bust to turn a lifetime of riches into dust. As I write this book, there is another reminder of how fleeting the money in our wallets can be, and that is inflation. (Nobel Prize-winning economist Milton Friedman once said, "Inflation is always and everywhere a monetary phenomenon"). Granted, the cost of living where you live may have dissipated by the time this book is released. However, it's fair to say that the years following the outbreak of COVID-19 brought about the worst cost of living crisis for a generation, as just about every corner of the globe experienced high levels of inflation not seen for about 30-40 years. Indeed, it's being called 'The Second Great Inflation' – no doubt in reference to the Great Inflation of the 1970s. But before we get into the world's recent spell of inflation and its past episodes – it's only fitting we first define what it is, and the best way of doing this is through an example. So imagine you and your family going to your local store where you do your regular shopping and notice that the prices of things you typically buy have increased. If the items in your shopping basket cost $90 last year and now cost $100 at a basic level, that's inflation.

Of course, we know that prices are changing constantly, but we don't say there is inflation every time we see a price increase. Instead, we say there is inflation when the prices of many things we buy rise simultaneously and continue to rise. Explained another way, inflation is ongoing increases in the general price level for goods and services in an economy over time.

Prices can change for different reasons and in different ways. The prices of individual goods and services, such as a car ride or a haircut, can vary because of the market forces of supply or demand. For example, the price of oranges can rise because of a frost in Florida, or parking can increase during a sporting event such as a World Cup Final or the Olympic Games because more people need parking spots. People often mistake these higher prices as examples of inflation – but that's not the case in the first place; these higher prices probably won't last for long. The prices of oranges and parking will most likely return to where they were once the supply and demand conditions change again.

However, traditional economics theory would dictate that there are two primary causes of sustained increases in prices. There is "Demand-Pull" and "Cost-Push" inflation. So, let's start by looking at the latter – cost-push inflation. This happens when the price of a business's inputs or raw materials (say oil or grain) goes up over time, and that could be because of anticipated events or unanticipated events, like a natural disaster. An excellent example of this would be what has happened to many of the world's economies coming out of lockdown following the onset of the COVID-19 global pandemic in the late embers of 2019. On the back of that, we saw global supply chain bottlenecks.

This is a scenario in which there is a significant disruption or slowdown in the flow of goods, materials, or components within a complex network of suppliers, manufacturers, distributors, and retailers that span multiple countries and regions. This disruption can lead to delays, shortages, and inefficiencies in the production and distribution of goods, impacting various industries and potentially causing economic challenges.

Take the example of a tech giant like Apple, which works with supplies in about 43 countries and six continents to make its iPhone, iPad, apple watches, apple TVs, etc. Or what about the commercial aircraft manufacturing giant like Boeing? A Boeing aeroplane has more than three million parts, including its engine, passenger entry doors, tail fin, and cargo access doors. The company's supply chain is a massive, global operation.

So although the company is based in Chicago, Illinois, USA, the firm has a supplier network that stretches around the globe and includes 12,000 active suppliers – more than 6,000 of them being small and diverse businesses located in countries like Japan, France, China, and Canada – all of them different continents. And so when many national governments signalled for lockdowns in the Spring of 2020, that meant companies like Apple and Boeing that need parts to be shipped in from their various supplies across the globe – faced longer lead times, resulting in a rise in shipping costs.

And now, because most of these inputs will go into the price of manufacturing their products, this inevitably leads to higher costs for the firms. So, what do firms do in response to this? They pass these costs onto consumers through higher prices to compensate for these higher costs. This is known as cost-push inflation.

Now, to be sure, there are other causes of cost-push inflation. Another excellent example of this is the ongoing war between Russia and Ukraine. Russia is a significant supplier of oil, gas, and metals, and Ukraine is one of the world's leading suppliers of wheat and corn – any disruptions in these supplies will cause food and energy prices to rise sharply – which is precisely what has happened. And so we learned earlier that when prices rise, it now costs more to buy the same basket of goods, meaning the purchasing power of money has fallen. The most brutal hit was those in low-income countries, where families spend around 42 per cent of their household incomes on food.

Indeed, in a 2022 report, the United Nations Development Programme (UNDP) concluded that some 71 million people worldwide experienced poverty due to soaring food and energy prices driven by Russia's invasion of Ukraine – with parts of Africa, the Balkans, and Asia being hardest hit. "The cost of living impact is almost without precedent in a generation ... and that is why it is so serious," said Achim Steiner, the UNDP administrator.[85]

Apart from cost-push inflation, there is also what economists call demand-pull inflation, which is when the demand for goods and services outpaces the ability of firms to supply those goods that are in demand. In other words, there are "too many dollars chasing too few goods." This tends to happen when the economy is strong or in a boom phase where incomes and consumer and business confidence are rising quickly.

Demand-pull is probably a better reflection of what happens when the economy is said to be close to total capacity – i.e., all its resources - land, labour, and capital are being used to their maximum. In the case of a very well-functioning economy, people may feel that they have more disposable income to spend, and therefore, demand for goods and services may go up. And if companies operate at total capacity, they won't be able to increase their production to keep up with that demand. So that could force them to raise prices.

---

[85] https://www.aljazeera.com/news/2022/7/7/inflation-pushed-71m-people-into-poverty-since-ukraine-war-undp

However, governments and central banks can also cause inflation. During times of economic hardship – like a recession when economic output is low and unemployment is high, politicians may feel the need to stimulate the economy. This can be spent on infrastructure projects like building new roads, railways, and ports. This, in turn, creates more jobs in the economy, leading to higher incomes and greater demand for goods and services, pushing up the price level.

On the other hand, the central bank might try to stimulate an economy by printing more money – usually digitally in what's known as quantitative easing or they typically would reduce interest rates, which represent the cost of borrowing and the reward for saving. The goal here is to get people to save less and borrow more – which will cause demand to rise faster than supply – which can only lead to higher prices. Now, it's important to note that there are other causes of inflation, such as inflation expectations – (where the anticipation of higher prices becomes a self-fulfilling prophecy), inflation caused by higher demand for a country's exports, and wage inflation – which happens when workers demand higher wages causing the production costs for businesses to rise which ends up leading to higher prices.

However, one potential cause of inflation that made the headlines in the spring of 2023 is called "greedflation."

So rather than inflation occurring due to the pandemic, the war in Russia and Ukraine, or a mismatch between demand and supply, the inflation we've experienced is due to profiteering by corporate businesses. Put simply, the relationship between the demand for and supply of goods and services has little to do with inflation. Instead, rising prices are a product of excess corporate power. According to Robert Reich, a former US secretary of labour and professor of public policy at the University of California, Berkeley, "Corporations have the power to raise prices without losing customers because they face so little competition." [86]

And they face so little competition because "since the 1980s, two-thirds of all American industries have become more concentrated." He goes on to say that Corporations are using those increasing costs – of materials, components, and labour – as excuses to raise their prices even higher, resulting in more significant profits. "This is why corporate profits are close to levels not seen in over half a century." Albert

---

[86] https://www.theguardian.com/commentisfree/2022/sep/25/inflation-price-controls-robert-reich

Edwards, a senior analyst at the French-based multinational financial services company Société Générale, agrees with Reich.

In an interview, he told the UK-based newspaper 'The Guardian that the rise in inflation to double digits in the Western world was made worse by greedflation. "Companies [have], under the cover of recent crises, pushed margins higher," he said in a note. "And, most surprisingly, they continue to do so, even as their raw material costs disappear. Consumers are still 'tolerating' this 'excuseflation,' possibly because excess [government] largesse has provided households with a buffer. "My view remains that headline inflation will collapse below zero as food and energy comparisons turn deeply negative this year. But beware corporate 'greedflation' still lurking in the undergrowth."

Taken together, whether inflation is caused by demand factors, cost factors, or the greed of big corporations, they all have one thing in common – they all lead to a fall in the purchasing power of money – again highlighting the fragility of money in this present age. What's worse is that for many workers, the problem is that the growth has not matched the recent surge in prices observed in major developed economies in wages.

Hence, at the time of this writing, half a million public sector workers in the UK, such as doctors, nurses, teachers, and rail workers, have taken strike action in response to low pay. Meanwhile, in its Global Wage Report in 2022[87], the International Labour Organization (ILO), a specialized agency of the United Nations that focuses on labour and employment issues, estimated that global monthly wages fell in real terms to – 0.9 per cent in the first half of 2022.

Mainly due to the increase in inflation that started in 2021, the organisation noted that this was the first negative global wage growth recorded since the first edition of the Global Wage Report in 2008. So what exactly do we mean by "real wages"?

A real wage is the hourly rate of pay that has been adjusted for inflation. Real wages take into account inflation, so show how much purchasing power a pay packet comparable to previous years. Real wages rise when nominal wages (which don't account for inflation) rise quicker than the inflation

---

[87] https://www.ilo.org/digitalguides/en-gb/story/globalwagereport2022-23

rate. So, for example, if nominal wages increase by 2 per cent in a given year and consumer prices rise by 5 per cent, then real wages would have fallen by 3 per cent.

Speaking to the BBC about wage stagnation in Britain, Torsten Bell, chief executive of the Resolution Foundation, said that the wage stagnation of the past decade and a half is "almost completely unprecedented." "Nobody who's alive and working in the British economy today has ever seen anything like this. "This is definitely not what normal looks like. This is what failure looks like," [88]he added.

The story of soaring prices between 2021 and 2023 and its simultaneous effect on real wages is analogous to what happened during chapter 1 of the Book of Haggai in the Old Testament. In this period, the Jewish people had returned from Babylonian exile and were rebuilding the temple in Jerusalem. However, no sooner had they started rebuilding, they started to neglect it – instead focusing on their own pursuits and prosperity rather than dedicating themselves to restoring the sacred place of worship.

---

[88] https://www.resolutionfoundation.org/press-releases/15-years-of-economic-stagnation-has-left-workers-across-britain-with-an-11000-a-year-lost-wages-gap/

Addressing them, the prophet says, "You have planted much but harvested little. You eat but are not satisfied. You drink but are still thirsty. You put on clothes but cannot keep warm." But notice his last statement; "*Your wages disappear as though you were putting them in pockets filled with holes!*" In the olden times, people would keep their money in bags. But what good is a money bag, purse, or wallet if it is full of holes? It simply means their money was running away as fast as it was earned. Sound familiar?

Now, surprisingly for some – but unsurprisingly for others- inflation has been around since the Bible recorded periods. For instance, when King Jehoram was the ruler of Israel, the Arameans launched an assault on the nation, resulting in a period of severe inflation for the Israelites. The Arameans were neighbouring people who had interactions and conflicts with the Israelites and other surrounding countries. The besiegement of the capital city caused a scarcity of essential products, leading to what we might now term "runaway inflation" as described here in 2 Kings 6:25, "A great famine arose in the city [Samaria], and the siege lasted so long that a donkey's head was sold for eighty pieces of silver, and a cup of dove's dung was sold for five pieces of silver."

As a result, King Jehoram was on the brink of surrendering to the Arameans.

However, the prophet Elisha encouraged the king to hold on for just one more day, countering the King's despair with a message from the Lord. "This is what the Lord says: By this time tomorrow, in the markets of Samaria, six quarts of fine flour will cost only one piece of silver, and twelve quarts of barley grain will cost only one piece of silver" (2 Kings 7:1, NLT).

This subsequently brought an end to the period of inflation in the land. Elsewhere, the Book of Deuteronomy gives us the first reference to price goring, now known as "greedflation." In the 25th chapter of Deuteronomy, Moses says in verses 13-16, "In all your transactions you must use accurate scales and honest measurements so that you will have a long, good life in the land the Lord your God is giving you. All who cheat with unjust weights and measurements are detestable to the Lord your God." In this passage, Moses refers to having one weight or measure heavier or more significant than the standard and another lighter or smaller. This deceptive practice allowed merchants at that time to charge more for the same quantity of goods or pay less when buying items. Such rules would lead to the exploitation of one party while benefiting the other – exactly what some corporations are being accused of doing through their prices. But perhaps, more strikingly, the Bible predicts that in the end times, the world will be gripped by inflation.

"When the Lamb opened the third seal, I heard the third living creature say, 'Come!' I looked, and there before me was a black horse! Its rider was holding a pair of scales in his hand. Then I heard what sounded like a voice among the four living creatures, saying, 'Two pounds of wheat for a day's wages, and six pounds of barley for a day's wages, and do not damage the oil and the wine!'"

The reality of inflation should remind us that riches are fleeting: "Cast but a glance at riches, and they are gone, for they will surely sprout wings and fly off to the sky like an eagle."

"The Wealth of the world has indeed increased by leaps and bounds, but most of it has fallen into the laps of the few"

- Ernest Howard Crosby.

"We are the 99 Percent"

ONCE, THERE LIVED a wealthy man who possessed an abundance of fine and fashionable purple clothing, enjoyed high-quality, sophisticated, and expertly prepared food daily, and resided in a large mansion. Just outside the gates of his luxurious home, there lay a destitute and homeless man named Lazarus, covered in unsightly skin lesions. He was so hungry that he longed to scavenge scraps from the rich man's trash. Dogs would come and lick the sores on his skin.

Eventually, Lazarus passed away; he was taken up by the angels to the lap of Abraham in Heaven. Subsequently, the wealthy man also died and was buried, finding himself in the realm of the dead. In his torment, he gazed up and saw Abraham with Lazarus in his embrace. Desperate for relief, the rich man called out to Abraham, pleading for mercy. He requested that Lazarus be sent to dip his fingertip in water to cool his burning tongue, tormented by the flames. But Abraham responded, reminding the rich man that he enjoyed abundant comfort and pleasure in his earthly life while Lazarus endured suffering and pain.

Their roles were reversed, with Lazarus finding comfort and the rich man experiencing agony. Furthermore, an unbridgeable divide separated the two realms, making it impossible for anyone to cross. Still, the wealthy man persisted and asked Abraham to send Lazarus to his father's house to warn his five brothers about the consequences of their path.

He hoped that such a warning would prevent them from ending up in torment as he did. Abraham, however, reasoned that the brothers had the law of Moses and the writings of the prophets to guide them, and they should heed those teachings. The rich man disagreed, believing his brothers would only change their ways if someone returned from the dead to warn them. In response, Abraham stated that if they were not attentive to Moses and the prophets, they would remain unconvinced even if someone were to return from the dead to warn them.[89]

---

[89] https://www.biblegateway.com/passage/?search=Luke%2016%3A19-31&version=MSG

Does this story sound familiar? It is, of course, one of the many parables that are found in the New Testament bible. The parable of the rich man and Lazarus is a compelling illustration of Jesus' teachings and has prompted numerous discussions on its meaning and interpretation. At first blush, this parable portrays the stark contrast between a wealthy man living in luxury and a destitute beggar found outside the gate of his mansion.

Jesus delivers essential lessons about the afterlife and our society today through this poignant narrative. Indeed, one could argue that it's one of the few overt references to one of the most dominant issues of today: income inequality - which we will look at later in this chapter. But going back to the parable – let's first set the stage for it by giving it some context.

The Rich Man and Lazarus parable is within a section of Luke's Gospel (Luke 15-16), where Jesus shares several parables about wealth, stewardship, and the Kingdom of God. To be specific – he taught the following: The parable of the lost sheep (Luke 15:4-7), the parable of the lost coin (Luke 15:8-10), the parable of the prodigal son (Luke 15:11-32), and the parable of the shrewd manager (Luke 16:1-13).

In fact, In the verses leading up to the parable, Jesus addresses the Pharisees and religious leaders of the time who were known for their love of money and material wealth. He criticizes their hypocrisy and lack of concern for the poor and marginalized. And so we come to these two characters in the story.

The first is a rich man, described as wearing fine purple linen. This is significant because purple symbolized royalty in the ancient world. After all, its dyes were rare and difficult to manufacture.

At the same time, fine linen was soft and comfortable as opposed to scratchy course clothing. It, too, was also the clothing of the rich and well-connected. The poor man, Lazarus, however, is less clothed in quite the same array. He's described as being covered with sores – so much so that even the dogs licked at his sores.

Furthermore, he was happy to eat the scraps that fell from the rich man's table – emphasizing the gulf in economic class between the two protagonists. Fast-forward a few years now, and both find themselves in the afterlife – with Lazarus resting with Abraham while the rich find themselves in torment. Other versions say that he was in "great pain."

Seeking to find a solution to his ills, he pleads for Lazarus to dip the end of his finger in water and cool his tongue to quench the anguish he finds himself in. This is quite a dramatic role reversal from earlier on in the story.

However, Abraham responds by reminding the rich man that in his lifetime, he (the rich man) enjoyed the blessings of prosperity, whereas Lazarus endured hardships. Before we go further in the analysis of this story, it's important to note that at this point, nowhere in the narrative is there any indication that the rich man had wronged his counterpart. Nor does the parable imply that money in and of itself is a sin. Instead, Abraham highlights the glaring contrast between their lives—the rich man lived comfortably while Lazarus endured torment.

The central sin in this tale lies in the rich man's apathy and indifference towards Lazarus; though he wasn't actively harmed – any compassion was absent. To the rich man, Lazarus is just another face in the crowd, an invisible poor person. Abraham further explains that there is a great "chasm" fixed between the two – again highlighting the exchange of roles from before. So what is the moral of the story – at least at this stage of the narrative?

Skip a few books of the New Testament, and you'll find a scripture in James 1:9-11 that says, "Any of God's people who are poor should be glad he thinks so highly of them. But those who are rich should boast about how God has brought them low and humbled them, for all their earthly glory will one day fade away like a wildflower in the meadow. For as the scorching heat of the sun causes the petals of the wildflower to fall off and lose its appearance of beauty, so the rich in the midst of their pursuit of wealth will wither away."

In other words, good people will have endless happiness, and their poverty and suffering will end. But those who are rich and cruel will face never-ending misery without any chance of getting help or forgiveness.

*****

Jesus' attempts to raise the consciousness of the *rich* about poverty, compassion, and social inequality are nothing new to society today. A little over a decade ago, Nobel Prize-winning economist Joseph Stiglitz claimed that the growing income disparity within numerous countries across the globe stands out as a "critical" challenge confronting the world today.

When writing his book, The Price of inequality, more than a fifth of all income in the United States went to the top 1%[90]. Indeed, according to Stiglitz, the United States had not experienced such a disparity since the period before the Great Depression in the 1930s, not to mention it is twice the proportion of 40 years ago.

In fact, in the aftermath of the Global Financial Crisis, when the U.S. economy returned to growth – 95% of the gains in income went to the top 1%. Even within this top 1%, he found that there was even inequality within this range, with ultra-high income earners in the top 0.1% taking home some 11.3% of total income in 2012, three to four times the number forty years ago. This gap between the rich and the poor caused widespread anger across most of the advanced world as many people felt that the financial industry, symbolized by Wall Street and the City of London, had benefited from government bailouts. At the same time, ordinary citizens suffered the consequences of the crisis, including job losses and foreclosures. This was, of course, compounded by the fact that those who had been bailed out had benefited most from the economic recovery. This led to

---

[90] https://www.pass.va/content/dam/casinapioiv/pass/pdf-volumi/acta/acta_19/es41-stiglitz.pdf

the creation of "The Occupy Wall Street" movement, a socio-political protest movement primarily focused on addressing income inequality, corporate influence over politics, and the perceived injustices of the global financial system. The rallying cry for these protesters became "we are the 99% - referencing the quantity of wealth held by the elite.

Filmmaker Michael Moore described Occupy Wall Street as being made up of those who "have lost their jobs, their homes, their *American Dreams*." It began in September 2011 in the financial district of New York City. It quickly gained national and international attention, sparking similar protests in other cities across the United States and worldwide. Inspired by the Arab Spring uprisings in 2011 and the Spanish Indignados movement, activists took to the streets to voice their grievances against social and economic inequalities.

The movement began in Adbusters, a Canadian anti-consumerist magazine, which first proposed the idea of Occupy Wall Street in July 2011[91]. They called for people to gather in New York City's financial district to protest

---

[91] https://www.npr.org/2011/10/20/141526467/exploring-occupy-wall-streets-adbuster-origins

corporate power and wealth disparities. And so on September 17, 2011, a group of about 1000 activists and protesters – primarily young - set up camp in Zuccotti Park, located near Wall Street in Lower Manhattan. The Park was considered a "privately owned public space" operated by Goldman Sachs – one of the banks the U.S. government had bailed out, so it made perfect sense for the group to use the park set-up shop.

Furthermore, the Occupy Wall Street movement at Zuccotti Park ensured that the protest gained tremendous visibility, making it impossible for anyone in that region of the city to miss the demonstrations. The Park had enjoyed considerable popularity among visitors before the protest. Still, when the demonstrators took over the space in the way that they did, their message loomed large, serving as a constant reminder to Wall Street workers who had to hustle their way through protesters to get to their offices.

Unsurprisingly, the movement initially faced scepticism and criticism from some media and political establishment segments, who questioned its goals and organization. However, the movement started gaining traction once celebrities such as Danny Glover, Mark Ruffalo, and Tim Robins began to join the movement.

Together, their persistence and widespread attention contributed to a shift in public discourse, bringing income inequality and corporate influence into the national conversation. But the OWS movement was significantly propelled when, in October of that year, approximately 700 demonstrators were taken into custody after participating in a march that spanned across the Brooklyn Bridge.

Some of the protesters are accusing the police of deliberately enticing and trapping them on the lower road level of the bridge. At the same time, the authorities maintain that they had warned the demonstrators to stay on the designated walkway level. Consequently, the massive number of arrests becomes the focal point of media attention, gracing the front pages of newspapers and leading TV news broadcasts. In fact, according to TIME magazine, Occupy started slowly, drawing in 2% of total news coverage by the end of its second week, as measured by the Pew Research Center. By mid-November, that number had grown steadily to 13%, driving economic issues to absorb almost a quarter of newscasts[92].

---

[92] https://time.com/6117696/occupy-wall-street-10-years-later/

At its peak, OWS was generating media attention roughly equivalent to nearly $1 million in free advertising nightly. Drawing inspiration from the Occupy Wall Street (OWS) movement, protests ignited in major urban centres such as Boston, Chicago, Los Angeles, and Seattle.

Occupy, Nobel laureate Joseph Stiglitz told TIME, "is part of a series of events that precipitate an understanding of the limitations of corporate America, something that today has morphed into a sense of the misdeeds not only by the financial sector, the fossil fuel sector, and now by big tech. It was the first critique that crystallized it compellingly. Subsequent movements built on growing understanding that the corporate sector is not serving American interests." [93]

One month later, to mark "Bank Transfer Day," demonstrators marched in front of prominent banks and financial institutions. Their objective was to encourage fellow Americans to transfer their funds from large corporate banks to smaller community credit unions.

Approximately 600,000 individuals withdrew their money from central banks in the preceding month, supporting the

---

[93] https://time.com/6117696/occupy-wall-street-10-years-later/

movement towards community-focused financial institutions[94]. Asked about at the time about OWS, President Obama said, "I think it expresses the frustrations the American people feel, that we had the biggest financial crisis since the Great Depression, huge collateral damage throughout the country... and yet you're still seeing some of the same folks who acted irresponsibly trying to fight efforts to crack down on the abusive practices that got us into this in the first place."

However, Herman Cain, a Republican presidential candidate, was not thrilled with the movement, saying, "Don't blame Wall Street, don't blame the big banks, if you don't have a job and you're not rich, blame yourself!"

Fifty-nine days into the protests – the movement came to a dramatic end when the New York Police Department, under the direction of Mayor Michael Bloomberg, conducted a raid at Zuccotti Park – citing that the attack was due to the planned cleaning of the Park.

During the operation, the police reportedly cleared the area of protesters, removing tarps and tents and placing them in

---

[94] https://www.reuters.com/article/us-bank-transfer-idUSTRE80Q1TU20120127

dumpsters. In his 2016 book, The End of Protest: A New Playbook for Revolution, Micah White, editor at the activist magazine Adbusters, who was credited as the one who started it all, wrote, "An honest assessment reveals that Occupy Wall Street failed to live up to its revolutionary potential: We did not bring an end to the influence of money on democracy, overthrow the corporatocracy of the 1 per cent or solve income inequality."

He concluded that the movement was "a constructive failure because the movement revealed underlying flaws in dominant and still prevalent theories of how to achieve social change through collective action."

However, the vast wealth disparity is a bigger problem than income inequality. Wealth in America is far more concentrated than income. At the time of writing his book, Stiglitz found that the wealthiest 1% of Americans held 35% of the wealth, and even more when housing wealth was not counted, and by 2021, the top 10% of households by net worth owned 70% of the country's wealth. Furthermore, according to the Urban Institute, from 1963 to 2013, families in the bottom 10 per cent of wealth ownership went from having no wealth on average to $2,000 in debt[95].

At this stage, it's essential to distinguish between income and wealth. Income is not the same as wealth. Income is not the same as wealth. Income is a flow of money going to the factors of production over some time.

So, for example, the wages received from working a job are counted as income as it flows to your account over time. The same goes for enterprise – any profits made from a successful business again flow to the business account over time. On the other hand, wealth is considered a "stock concept "– a large amount of money or valuable possessions that can be held by a person, group, or country at a specific time.

Examples of this would be the ownership of property, savings in a bank account, and the ownership of shares in a business. Therefore, earning an income is a relatively

---

[95] https://www.urban.org/policy-centers/cross-center-initiatives/inequality-and-mobility/projects/wealth-inequalities#:~:text=families%20near%20the%20bottom%20of,percentile)%20quadrupled%20their%20wealth%2C%20and

straightforward matter, primarily revolving around wages and compensation.

In contrast, wealth exhibits a more dynamic and diverse nature. Assets like real estate, stocks, and bonds can increase in value over time, making one even wealthier. However, the influence of wealth runs much deeper. Ownership of land or buildings allows significant control over how it is used.

Likewise, possessing someone else's debt grants considerable legal power over their livelihood. Additionally, holding shares in a company allows you to exert influence over its governance, including decisions regarding investments, hiring policies, and remuneration practices. While income determines one's present standard of living, wealth empowers individuals to shape the economy's fabric and future direction.

What's more, because the ownership of assets brings forth income, it means that you can then use it to buy even more income-bearing assets. As a result, we often observe an unending cycle of wealth passing down through successive generations within the confines of the same family. In other words, the rich get richer, so wealth inequality is worse than income inequality.

According to economist Derrick Hamilton, "Wealthier families are better positioned to afford elite education, access capital to start a business, finance expensive medical procedures, reside in higher-amenity neighbourhoods, exert political influence through campaign contributions, purchase better legal representation, leave a bequest, and withstand financial hardship resulting from an emergency." [96]

Now, to be sure, some will argue that this wealth is justified as "just deserts" for the significant contributions that these individuals have made. If we look at those at the top, they are not those who have made the crucial innovations that have transformed our economies and societies; they are not the discoverers of DNA, the laser, and the transistor; not the brilliant individuals who made the discoveries without which we would not have had the modern computer.

Disproportionately, they are those who have excelled in rent-seeking, in wealth appropriation, in figuring out how to get a larger share of the nation's pie rather than enhancing the size of that pie. (Such rent-seeking activity typically results

---

[96] https://www.stlouisfed.org/-/media/project/frbstl/stlouisfed/files/pdfs/hfs/20160525/papers/hamilton-paper.pdf

in the size of the economic pie shrinking from what it otherwise would be).

Among the most notable are those in the financial sector, some of whom made their wealth by market manipulation, engaging in abusive credit card practices, predatory lending, and moving money from the bottom and middle of the income pyramid to the top.

So, too, a monopolist makes his money by contracting output from what it otherwise would be, not by expanding it. The Great Recession showed the ineptness of the "just deserts" argument. In no small measure, this recession was caused by the financial sector, which is responsible for so much of the inequality today. Even as they were bringing their firms and the global economy to the brink of ruin, the managers of these firms walked off with multimillion-dollar bonuses.

As a result, there is a temptation for those considered to be in the top 1% to be high-minded and arrogant. However, the writer of Proverbs strictly warns that "One man considers himself rich, yet has nothing (to keep permanently); another man considers himself poor, yet has great (and indestructible) riches."

Put another way, when compared to the external realm, wealth holds little if any value at all, whereas as we saw with the beggar Lazarus – who I'm sure would consider himself as being part of the 99 per cent – he had the indestructible riches of eternal life in heaven compared to the rich man who was in constant torment. Indeed, a rich man's wealth to him is like a "strong city," says the writer, and like a "high wall" in his imagination.

One version of the same passage says, "The rich think their wealth protects them; they imagine themselves safe behind it." This is similar again to the parable of the foolish rich man that we noted earlier, whose arrogance thought that his great wealth and harvest were his protection until his life was required.

This is why the Apostle Paul also adds to the warning of the writer of Proverbs by saying the following, "Tell those who are rich not to be proud and not to trust in their money, which will soon be gone, but their pride and trust should be in the living God who always richly gives us all we need for our enjoyment."

And so what can those who are wealthy do not only to help solve the issue of income and wealth inequality but, more importantly, have wealth that lives beyond this earth that we are in? Paul says they need to use their money to do good – being rich in good works, for example, happily to those in need.

By doing this, he says, they will be "storing up real treasure for themselves in heaven—it is the only safe investment for eternity!" Therefore, the following chapter will look at those rich men and women who have heeded the call of giving to the needy and whether or not it is easier for a camel to pass through the eye of a needle than for a rich man to enter the Kingdom of Heaven

"Wealth is not to feed our egos but to feed the hungry and help people help themselves"

- Andrew Carnegie.

The Gospel of Wealth

WHETHER IT'S THE 2008 financial crisis, the dot-com bubble in the early 2000s, the Asian stock market crash in the mid-1990s, or Black Monday in 1987, history has all but confirmed what the Apostle Paul says in 1 Timothy 6:17 – that riches have an "uncertainty" about them.

They are, for a better term, "here today and gone tomorrow." Indeed, in the book of Matthew, Jesus tells his followers not to lay up treasures on earth for themselves because, amongst other things, thieves can break in and steal them. One only has to look at the number of times robbers have broken into the homes of wealthy sportsmen and women either to steal cash, expensive jewellery, or valuable memorabilia.

And so, given the above, what should be your approach to the wealth you have, given its unpredictable nature? In other words, how can you acquire eternal wealth that lasts forever? Paul gives the most essential advice on this issue: If you are rich, you must use your money to do good. You should be rich in good works and give happily to those in need, always being ready to share with others and be "extravagantly" generous, as the writer of the Message Bible puts it.

By doing so, he says, you will be storing up real treasure for yourself in heaven—"It is the only safe investment for eternity!" One could even say that giving to the needy is not only for the material benefit of those who receive the wealth passed down but also for the spiritual enrichment of the giver- in this case, the rich.

But it's fair to say that over time, the wealthy – whether made rich because of the recent tech boom or their involvement in financial markets, are giving money away at unprecedented levels and engaging increasingly in Philanthropy.

In fact, despite COVID-19 and the economic downturn that followed for most of the developed and developing world, 25 of the most generous philanthropists in the United States donated $27 billion to charitable causes in 2022, according to a report by Forbes Magazine[97]. The total amount given in 2022 was more than the two years combined ($20 billion)

---

[97] https://www.forbes.com/sites/forbeswealthteam/2023/01/23/americas-top-givers-2023-the-25-most-philanthropic-billionaires/?sh=242dc2b22e9e

and double the sum donated in 2018. According to Forbes's estimates, the nation's 25 biggest donors have already parted with $196 billion. Warren Buffet, for instance, gave $5.4 billion to various charities in 2022 and has donated $51.5 billion to date.

Bill Gates and Melinda French Gates, despite their 2021 divorce, collectively gave $38.4 billion. Google co-founder Sergey Brin and hedge funder Ken Griffin provided $2.55 billion and $1.56 billion in 2022, respectively. What's more interesting about this report is that these philanthropists have seen their fortunes shrink.

According to the same Forbes report, the world's wealthiest people lost $2 trillion in 2022. Furthermore, the estimated combined wealth of the top 25 philanthropists dropped by 15 per cent ($164 billion) year-over-year to $936 billion in 2022. So, seen in this way, the generosity to those in need is commendable. But it's not just wealthy billionaires engaging in charitable giving: Corporate America is also getting increasingly involved in Philanthropy.

For example, to date, America's 50 biggest public companies and their foundations collectively committed at least $49.5 billion since Floyd's murder three years to addressing racial inequality — an amount that appears unequalled in sheer scale. Indeed, going back to 2021, corporate giving in the U.S. alone is estimated to have exceeded $21 billion.

So, what exactly is Philanthropy? According to the Merriam-Webster dictionary, it means goodwill to fellow members of the human race. The Greek root of Philanthropy is literally translated as "loving people." The English word can refer to general goodwill to one's fellow people, as well as to the active effort to promote the welfare of people. Still, in our modern times, it is most often used to refer specifically to the practice of giving money and time to help make life better for others – particularly for those who are less well off. However, historically, if we go back Two thousand years, we find that there were different views regarding charitable giving and helping those in need.

For example, the ancient Romans felt no obligation to the poor. For the Romans, the poor were socially invisible. Wealthy Romans gave to the public to display their incredible generosity—but this was always done with an expectation of receiving honour and glory in return. Put another way, they weren't always helping people experiencing poverty for the right reasons.

But the ancient Jews, in contrast, felt a responsibility to help the suffering and disadvantaged. Sin, they knew, creates debt with God, and so they thought that by helping those in need, they could store up treasure in heaven.

Things, however, started to change at the turn of the 15th century and heading into the 16th century as the culture of the medieval world disappeared, meaning its economic, political, and social structures also faded along with it. A new social fabric emerged that saw towns and cities emerge as significant centres of influence – replacing the era of what was known as "rural feudalism," which meant that landowners were no longer mutually obliged to peasants.

As a result, Feudal lords no longer protected the welfare of their dependents, which released peasants from their duty to stay and serve. In Europe, for instance, the dissatisfaction with the practices and teachings of the Roman Catholic Church and the corruption within the church hierarchy created a desire for religious reform.

As a result, it marked a period of profound change in the Christian church in Europe. It led to the establishment of many Protestant denominations, which diverged from the Roman Catholic Church. In the Middle East, the Ottoman

Empire, an Islamic superpower, reached its peak, while powerful dynasties governed China and Japan in East Asia. On a global scale, the Age of Discovery sparked an unprecedented exchange of people, goods, ideas, and cultures.

The period is characterized as a time when Europeans began exploring the world by sea in search of new trading routes, wealth, and knowledge. These transformative developments impacted the evolution of modern Philanthropy as the focus shifted toward urban areas, altering the dynamics of giving and receiving.

Moreover, during this era, the world experienced significant upheaval through wars and revolutions, presenting Philanthropy with new challenges. Military conflicts like the Napoleonic Wars and the American Revolution not only resulted in displaced persons, widows, and orphans but also led to the establishment of new nations that were tasked with improving the welfare of their citizens. Simultaneously, the advent of industrialization brought its own set of difficulties due to rapid urbanization.

The deplorable living conditions in overcrowded tenements and factories sparked discussions about sanitation and workers' rights. The issue of abolishing slavery also reached a critical juncture, eventually culminating in a violent civil war in the United States. While the decline of slavery was observed, colonial empires emerged, disrupting the social fabric of both colonies and colonizers. Amidst this tumultuous period, a need arose to address questions regarding enhancing human well-being.

Consequently, a dual system of Philanthropy emerged, characterized by courageous private initiatives aimed at reform and an increased public obligation to support those in need. The upheavals of the 19th century, which included the abolishment of slavery in much of Europe and the Americas and the continuation of the Industrial Revolution – produced massive social consequences.

This required philanthropists to respond to the immediate needs of society. And the first philanthropist to understand this was Andrew Carnegie. He was born on November 25, 1835, in Dunfermline, Fife, Scotland. Although the town had been known as Scotland's medieval capital, Carnegie grew up during a period when it started to see a downturn in economic fortunes[98].

---

[98] https://www.biography.com/business-leaders/andrew-carnegie

One of those who were hit hardest by this was Andrew's father, a handloom weaver, a profession the young Carnegie was expected to follow. Despite enjoying a reputation for producing the finest damask linens in Great Britain, the introduction and widespread use of steam-powered looms due to the Industrial Revolution rendered the need for humans- including Andrew's dad- to oversee the weaving process.

This then forced his mother into the workforce to support the family. She decided to open a small grocery shop and mending shoes. "I began to learn what poverty meant," Carnegie once wrote, "It was burnt into my heart then that my father had to beg for work. And then and there came the resolve to cure that when I got to be a man."

Amid their struggles, Carneige's mother, Margaret, set her sights on moving the family abroad to America to escape poverty in Scotland. And so, in 1848, the family arrived in Pittsburgh. There, Carnegie's father secured work in a cotton factory, while Andrew took a position in the same building as a bobbin boy, earning $1.20 a week.

Bobbin Boys became a crucial fixture in the early Industrial Revolution. These children were responsible for changing the bobbins in textile machinery, which required them to crawl under the machinery and replace the filled bobbins with empty ones.

However, Carnegie's stint in the factory only lasted for a week as he took up the task of being a messenger boy in the city's telegraph office at age 14, with the story going that he was able to memorize Pittsburgh's street layout as well as the names and addresses of the important people he delivered to.

One of the keys to his later success was one of the men he met at the telegraph office: Thomas A. Scott. Then, beginning his career at Pennsylvania Railroad, Scott was impressed by the young Carnegie. He offered him a job in 1853 as his private secretary and personal telegrapher at $35 a month at 18 years old. Always enthusiastic about embracing fresh responsibilities, Carnegie progressively ascended the ranks within the Pennsylvania Railroad, eventually assuming the role of superintendent for the Pittsburgh Division after succeeding Scott.

With the onset of the Civil War, Scott was enlisted to oversee military transportation for the Union, and Carnegie served as his chief assistant throughout this period. Indeed, the Civil War played a significant role in fuelling the iron industry due to increased demand for weapons and ammunition, railroads and transportation, and shipbuilding.

And so, sensing the opportunity to make significant gains, Carnegie departed from the Pennsylvania Railroad despite earning substantial sums of money. In 1865, he established the Keystone Bridge Company, which was dedicated to replacing wooden bridges with more robust iron alternatives. Within two years, he achieved an impressive yearly income of $5000. By 33, he earned *$50,000 a year* and had a net worth of $400,000. After acquiring the Keystone Bridge Company, Andrew Carnegie invested heavily in the steel industry.

From about 1872–73, at about age 38, he began concentrating on steel, founding the J. Edgar Thomson Steel Works, which would eventually evolve into the Carnegie Steel Company. In the 1870s, Carnegie's new company built the first steel plants in the United States to use the new Bessemer steelmaking process, borrowed from Britain. In 1889, Carnegie's vast holdings were consolidated into the Carnegie Steel Company, a limited partnership that dominated the American steel industry. In 1890, the

American steel industry's output surpassed Great Britain's for the first time, mainly owing to Carnegie's successes[99].

In 1900, the profits of Carnegie Steel (which became a corporation) were $40,000,000, of which Carnegie's share was $25,000,000. Subsequently, in 1901, Carnegie opted to sell his company to the freshly established United States Steel Corporation, helmed by J.P. Morgan (who eventually himself would become another successful philanthropist), for a substantial sum of $480,000,000.

Following this strategic business manoeuvre, Carnegie embraced retirement, channelling his energy and considerable resources into his expansive philanthropic endeavours – starting with a famous editorial piece. Originally titled "Wealth" and published in the June 1889 edition of the North American Review, Carnegie produced what is now considered a foundational document in Philanthropy. He noticed at the time that "the problem of our age is the administration of wealth, so that the ties of brotherhood may still bind together the rich and poor in harmonious relationship."

---

[99] https://www.pbs.org/wgbh/americanexperience/features/carnegie-biography/

Acknowledging that the conditions of human life have not only been changed but revolutionized, he said, "This, then, is held to be the duty of the man of Wealth... becoming the mere agent and trustee for his poorer brethren, bringing to their service his superior wisdom, experience, and ability to administer, doing for them better than they would or could do for themselves." He argues that even though wealth accumulation is inevitable, it can benefit society's progress and that the wealthy have a moral obligation to use their wealth for the greater good.

Carnegie's philanthropic career began in the 1870s. While he backed numerous initiatives and supported various causes, his most renowned contributions were providing costless public library structures. Besides supporting libraries, Carnegie financed thousands of church organizations nationwide and worldwide. His vast wealth was pivotal in establishing numerous colleges, schools, non-profit organizations, and associations in his adopted country and beyond.

One of his most notable and impactful contributions was the creation of several trusts and institutions that bear his name, including the Carnegie Museums of Pittsburgh, the Carnegie Trust for the Universities of Scotland, Carnegie Institution for Science, Carnegie Foundation (which supports the Peace Palace), Carnegie Dunfermline Trust, Carnegie Foundation for the Advancement of Teaching, Carnegie Endowment for International Peace, and the Carnegie UK Trust.

These institutions benefited from his monetary contributions and carried his lasting influence. During his lifetime, Carnegie had a peak, inflation-adjusted net worth of $310 billion. That's enough to make him the 4th richest human of all time.

Andrew Carnegie will go down as one of the most generous philanthropists in human history, having donated over 90% of his fortune to various foundations, charities, and organizations before his death. Ultimately, he believed that "The man who dies rich dies disgraced." Nevertheless, Carnegie wasn't alone in pioneering philanthropic efforts in the early 20th century. Alongside him was one John D. Rockefeller.

John was the second of six children born in 1839 in Richford, New York. Like the Carnegie family, the Rockefeller family also moved around a bit. From New York, they moved to Cleveland, Ohio. A keen mathematician, his father pushed him to pursue business, so he attended a three-month commercial education program that taught him bookkeeping and banking practices.

During his teenage years, at sixteen, he embarked on a career as a clerk within a commission house. This establishment dealt with buying and selling futures contracts, which are commitments to trade goods at a later date. Three years later, having garnered the trust of many influential business figures and bankers in Cleveland, just like Carnegie, he resigned from his clerk position and, in partnership with his neighbour Maurice Clark, established a business aimed at the handling of various goods such as grain, hay, meats, and other assorted products.

With both partners pooling their resources, they kickstarted the enterprise with a combined investment of $2,000 - calling themselves Clark & Rockefeller. Rockefeller's business found small success, helped by the rise of shipments of agricultural produce to industrial centres and a heavy demand for foodstuffs from Europe during the American Civil War.

At the end of the first year of business, they made a revenue of $450,000, a profit of $4,400 in 1860, and a profit of $17,000 the following year. However, when the oil industry began gaining traction in the 1860s, he saw the opportunity to compete with other businesses. So, in 1865, he invested in an oil refinery business.

Despite taking out a big loan to expand the refinery and taking on new partners to help him build up the business, his refinery produced at least twice as much oil as any other in Cleveland by the end of their first year in business. Indeed, three years later, it was the biggest oil refinery in the world.

Not long after this, on January 10, 1870, Rockefeller, alongside five other partners, formed the Standard Oil Company of Ohio. It held about 10% of the oil business when it was created. Here, Rockefeller devised a plan for consolidating all oil refining firms into one great firm to eliminate excess capacity and price-cutting. By the close of the decade, the Standard Oil Company did about 90 per cent of the refining in the United States, with almost 70 per cent being exported overseas. Rockefeller achieved all of this by the age of 40 [100].

---

[100] https://guides.loc.gov/this-month-in-business-history/january/standard-oil-established#:~:text=In%201870%2C%20Rockefeller%20joined%20in,than%20oil%20exploration%20and%20drilling.

During 1891-92, it was suggested that Rockefeller had a partial nervous breakdown from overwork. Rockefeller's activities were philanthropic from the mid-1890s until he died in 1937. Rockefeller's fortune peaked in 1912 at almost $900,000,000, but by then, he had already given away hundreds of millions of dollars.

On why he gave away so much of his wealth, Rockefeller was quoted as telling the New York Times that his exploits had been formed out in Ohio under the ministration of a dear old minister who preached, 'get money, get it honestly, and then give it wisely.'

****

The philanthropic efforts of Andrew Carnegie and John D. Rockefeller are great examples of rich men who used their wealth to help those in need -and both mostly done from pure motives. Today, however, there has been widespread criticism that many wealthy individuals and Corporate America are becoming more strategic in their Philanthropy.

Put another way, the giving today is not like the giving of yesterday, where individuals aren't necessarily always giving because they want to see those at the bottom rising to the top. Increasingly, Philanthropy is used as a form of public relations or advertising, promoting a person's or company's image or brand.

And so, at first blush, it is commendable that the old and new generations of philanthropists recognize that all their accumulated wealth has no place being hoarded and instead finds better use for good works and to help those in need. To be sure, it is argued these men and women have chosen "a good reputation over great riches," as the writer of Proverbs states (Proverbs 22:1).

But of course, in reference to Jesus's exchange with the young rich ruler, this is just one step in this exchange, which can be found in Matthew 19. In it, a wealthy young man seeks guidance from Jesus on how to inherit eternal life. Jesus advises him to follow the commandments, and the young man claims he has done so.

However, when Jesus challenges him to sell his possessions and follow Him, the young man is saddened because he's attached to his wealth. Jesus uses this encounter to teach about the challenges of material wealth and the importance of prioritizing God over possessions. And so yes, while the likes of Warren Buffet, Bill Gates, and Mark Zuckerberg may not have the same issue of this young rich ruler who found it hard to depart with his great wealth, the other part of following Jesus is the most pertinent issue for philanthropists in this present age.

You see, it'll be a terrible shame for someone to have all the riches in the world – and to do such good deeds towards society and give all their wealth away to those in poverty and yet still not submit to the salvation of Jesus. This is because good deeds – whether done by the poor or rich unfortunately will not get man into heaven. Neither can man buy their way into heaven, no matter how rich they are. The only way to heaven is through confessing and believing in Jesus Christ as your Lord and personal saviour alongside doing these good works because "By doing this they will be storing up real treasure for themselves in heaven—it is the only safe investment for eternity!

And they will be living a fruitful Christian life down here as well," writes Apostle Paul in (1 Timothy 6:19.) Therefore, if you are reading this book and have not yet surrendered your life to Jesus, please do so because once you do, God richly provides you with everything you can ever need.

What good is it for someone to gain the whole world yet forfeit their soul? Or what can anyone give in exchange for their soul?

- **Mark 8:36-37**

Greatest Opportunity Cost

IT'S A FRIDAY evening after a long work week, and you and your partner have set aside a little money to do something fun for the night. You can choose between watching the latest sequel of Harrison Ford's Indiana Jones or going to a restaurant for dinner. The option you decide not to choose would be what economists call your "opportunity cost." If the pair of you chose dinner, the opportunity cost would be the price of the meal plus what you both gave up by not going to the cinema. (It's important to note that whenever we purchase something, we pay two costs: the price we pay for it and the cost of what we have given up to acquire it.)

Similarly, with our money, if we choose to invest it, our opportunity cost will be not having saved it; if we decide to keep it, our opportunity cost will be not having invested it. Understanding opportunity cost is helpful because we can know what we will no longer gain by making a particular selection. By keeping that in mind, we can make better decisions.

The concept of opportunity cost is deeply rooted in basic economics. According to economists, our resources on this earth are scarce ("limited" in layman's terms). For example, at any one time, we can only use so much land, so many manufacturing plants, so much steel, so many workers, and so many entrepreneurs. (We call these the four factors of production: land, labour, capital, and enterprise.) However, this is juxtaposed against the number of things we desire to have – which can be endless, from clothes, cars, jewellery, property, and money, to name but a few.

Simply put, our needs are limited, while our wants are unlimited. We would always like more and better housing, more and better education - more and better of practically everything, but the simple fact is that the earth doesn't have the resources to meet all our wants and needs. Wouldn't it be lovely to live in a world where our resources were unlimited? Society could say yes to each of their wants - and there would sadly be no economists! (Some may say this is not a bad thing) But the stark reality is that we cannot say yes to everything because our resources are limited. To say yes to one thing requires saying no to another (remember that key term from earlier on, 'opportunity cost'). Whether we like it or not, we must make choices, as scarcity prohibits us from spending and saving the same dollar.

Let's take an example:

Consider a piece of land or greenery in your local community. This land presents us with several alternative uses. A local council could build a range of houses and flats on it. Alternatively, they could place a school & nursery on it. They could even create a small park on it. Indeed, they could leave the land undeveloped to maintain biodiversity and wildlife. But suppose the council decided the parcel of land should be used for housing. Should it be a large and expensive house or several modest ones to make it affordable for its local citizens? Suppose it is to be extensive and costly housing.

Who should live in the house? If the Halls live in it, the Williams family cannot afford it because their combined household income cannot afford it. There are alternative uses of the land in terms of the type of use and the sense of who gets to use it. The fact that land is scarce means that society must make choices concerning its use – bringing us back to opportunity costs. Now, not all opportunity costs are created equal. Your opportunity costs are not the same as the person next door.

What's more, we might not consider lost studying time or $6.50 spent on a smoothie instead of a milkshake as costly life decisions, but what about more significant choices—like the decision to either go to college or take up full-time employment or whether or not you should marry your high school sweetheart? To better understand the opportunity costs, we must consider two main factors. The first is our circumstances. Second, perhaps more importantly for those reading this book, is our view of what happens in the next life.

Often, when we are weighing up the choices we make in life, our circumstances dictate the value we place on the thing we've decided to miss out on in our decision. Sometimes, we don't have enough time to calculate costs and weigh the pros and cons, which often leads us to make hasty decisions. Other times, we cannot feel or see the costs and benefits in the short term.

Take Bill Gates. Having dropped out of a prestigious college like Harvard after only two years, he ended up masterminding one of the most successful software and technology businesses in Microsoft.

In his case, Bill's opportunity cost was graduating with a college education at Harvard and then working for a top firm on Wall Street or Corporate America.

However, his decision to bet on himself & his entrepreneurial spirit turned out to be the best choice he ever could've made. (Notwithstanding that, there was no way that Gates could've imagined the success he and Microsoft would have.)

Therefore, the value he placed on the opportunity cost of staying in college and working in the private sector was nothing compared to the importance he placed on becoming a billionaire at the helm of one of the largest companies in the world, Microsoft.

Now, to be sure, his circumstances may have played a massive role in his decision in that perhaps if things didn't go well on the entrepreneurial side – he had the fortunes of his mother's family to fall back on, and so viewed from this perspective one could argue that dropping out of college and reneging on a college degree wasn't much of an opportunity cost at all for Gates.

However, you can take someone like Ana Barros. President of the Harvard College First Generation back in 2016, Ana's family lived in a modest house bought from Habitat for Humanity (a non-profit organization that helps needy families.)

Her parents, who immigrated to the New York area from Colombia, barely had enough groceries to get by and lived where the sound of blaring police sirens was commonplace. Describing her first few years at Harvard, she explained in an interview with The Boston Globe newspaper that she might as well have had the words "low income" written on her forehead. "All you see are class markers everywhere, from how you dress to how you talk…You'd get weeded out of friendships based on what you could afford. If someone said let's go to the Square for dinner and see a movie, you'd move on."[101]

So imagine the thought of Ana returning home after her sophomore year at Harvard and telling her parents that she wants to throw in the towel, go off, and start her own business. Given her family's circumstances, such a decision

---

[101] https://news.harvard.edu/gazette/story/2016/02/a-stronger-sense-of-belonging/

would not be a moot option. Dropping out wasn't an option – indeed, the opportunity cost of such a choice would have been far more significant than Bill Gates's. So, these two cases are great examples of how our situations determine how we view the options we forgo/sacrifice when deciding. This brings us to perhaps the greatest opportunity cost in life. In comparing the value of the things we sacrifice, there's none as crucial as the choice we make about the eternity of our soul. During an exchange with his disciples and a crowd of his believers, Jesus Christ in the New Testament Bible says:

"Whoever wants to be my disciple must deny themselves, take their cross, and follow me. Whoever wants to save their life[b] will lose it, but whoever loses their life for me and the gospel will save it. What good is it for someone to gain the whole world yet forfeit their soul? Or what can anyone give in exchange for their soul?" (Matthew 16:24-26)

And so, in other words, there's an exchange or an opportunity cost of gaining the whole world (perhaps being a millionaire/billionaire who can buy whatever you want or need) – and that's your soul. So you ask: What is your soul?

The soul comprises three parts—the mind, the will, and the emotion. When it comes to mind, we know that the mind is where knowledge and wisdom are stored and acquired over time. Indeed, this is proven to be true in the Book of Proverbs, a book of the Christian Old Testament, in which the writer states, "For wisdom will enter your heart, and knowledge will be pleasant to your soul." (Proverbs 2:10).

According to the National Library of Medicine, the mind is the seat of the faculty of reason or the aspect of intellect and consciousness.

The Merriam-Webster dictionary defines will as "the power of control over one's actions or emotions." It also states that close synonyms include desire, wish, and choice. Therefore, your Will denotes fixed and persistent intent or purpose whenever you choose. For example, I'm sure you've heard the phrase, "Where there's a will, there's a way."

A prime casing point is Martin Luther King, whose will was to see a world where the colour of their skin would not judge their children but by their character's content. And he willed it to happen through the civil rights movement.

And using the Bike as a guide again, Job 7:15 says that the soul chooses. To choose something is a decision made by the act of the will. This proves that the choice must be a part of the soul. Job 6:7 says that the soul refuses. To choose and refuse are both functions of the will.

First Chronicles 22:19 says, "Set your...soul to seek." Just as we set our minds to think, we put our souls to seek. This is the soul deciding, proving that our will must be a part of the soul.

Then, finally, our emotions – which are classed as feelings such as happiness, love, fear, anger, or hatred- can be caused by the situation you are in or the people you are with. And so, by now, you'll understand that it's out of our knowledge (mind), will, and emotions that we make choices and decisions – our soul, in other words.

Now, depending on your belief system, you might believe that this soul –which there's no denying that you have - will just fade away like your body when you die. Put another way – once you die, your soul dies also.

Or perhaps you believe that once you die, your soul gets reincarnated into someone or something else, and the cycle continues forever until you become one with the universe.

Or maybe you think that once you die, your soul will live in some shadowy underworld where you'll roam the earth but be invisible to those who are alive in the world – and that your soul is confined to that reality. Indeed, there are endless views on the afterlife that one could write a whole book on. However, one cannot deny this straightforward fact, and that is – for those of us who are alive, we cannot honestly know what will happen to us when we die.

Nevertheless, we know of one man in history who died and came back to life and knows exactly what's waiting for us after we die – and that is Jesus Christ. According to the Four Gospels (Matthew, Mark, Luke & John) in the New Testament Bible, this man Jesus was crucified to death on a Cross and three days later rose again and appeared before his disciples and his followers.

In the years before he died and in the days after he rose again, there were many references to Heaven – for example, in Matthew 7:21, Jesus says, "Not everyone who says to Me, 'Lord, Lord,' shall enter the kingdom of Heaven, but he who does the will of My Father in Heaven." While about Hell, he says, "Don't fear those who kill the body," Jesus said, "rather fear Him who can destroy both soul and body in hell"

(Matt 10:28; see also 5:29-30; 23:15,33; Luke 10:15; 16:23)."

And so your view of eternity matters because it influences choices you make here and on earth and the opportunity costs, too. Indeed, every thought of the afterlife contradicts the other, so only one can be right. So the question for you as you read this – is which one do you believe? As I referenced earlier – what would it profit a man to gain the whole world yet forfeit his soul?

Suppose you do not believe in a Heaven & Hell. In that case, you may be one of the wealthiest men or women in the latest Forbes 100 list, or you may be a titan in the music, finance, corporate, and technology industry – indeed, you may have gained the whole world – the riches and the recognition but at what cost? I call it the greatest opportunity cost – your soul.

Your soul has two destinations: either Heaven or Hell. No amount of money can get your soul into Heaven – the Bible even states, "Or what can man exchange for his soul?" In truth, "No one can serve two masters, for either he will hate and love the other or be devoted to the one and despise the other. You cannot serve God and money."

One carries the reward of Heaven while the love of the other has far more trouble than the paper written on it.

Think of it from this perspective: What is the safest investment you could make here on earth? I'm sure a few financial assets might spring to mind, such as Gold, government bonds, savings, pension funds, and real estate. To be sure, they are all reasonable investments, so let's look at a few of them. Take Gold, for example, which is traditionally seen as an asset that holds value. This is because its prices tend to move independently of other investment markets, which can help protect our money when markets are volatile.

"Gold investments are seen as a hedge against inflation due to their historic use as a store of value dating back thousands of years and the relatively limited metal supply. As inflation hot up, Gold has risen dramatically in price," says Susannah Streeter of UK-based investment firm Hargreaves Lansdown.[102]

---

[102] https://www.thetimes.co.uk/money-mentor/article/is-gold-a-good-investment/#:~:text=%E2%80%9CGold%20investments%20are%20seen%20as,in%20a%20time%20of%20crisis.

Indeed, a 2023 Gallup poll shows that the percentage of Americans who name Gold the best long-term investment option has nearly doubled since last year, from 15% to 26%.[103] Gold tends to be the beneficiary when confidence levels in real estate and stocks are down," the poll report reads. "This is typical during times of economic recession or uncertainty, as happened around the time of the Great Recession, and is happening again today."

But what happens when times are good, and the economy is booming? Well, as you might have guessed, its value often stagnates or falls – meaning it's not as bulletproof as you think. Not to mention its ability to be stolen. Though rare in present times, there have been many times when Gold vaults have been raided.

On November 26, 1983, for instance, three tonnes of solid gold bullion was taken by six armed robbers from the Brink's-Mat security depot near Heathrow Airport in the UK. The criminals had been looking to do a run-of-mill heist

---

[103] https://news.gallup.com/poll/505592/real-estate-lead-best-investment-shrinks-gold-rises.aspx

when they stumbled across a much bigger prize of gold worth £26 million.[104]

What about the savings in your checking account (or current account if you're in the UK)? On the surface – it's not as volatile as Gold – as your savings' value doesn't necessarily align with the economic cycle. However, in times of inflation, your savings risk losing value in 'real' terms as you can buy less with your money.

Moreover, if we think back to the early part of 2023 when dozens of American customers were lined up outside of First Republic Bank, Silicon Valley Bank (SVB), and Signature Bank due to the threat of the potential loss of their savings should their banks fold in bankruptcy. So again, savings accounts are only safe to a certain extent.

Finally, let's look at real estate. Unlike Gold, which tends to see its value fall during times of economic prosperity, the value of real estate tends to rise when we are at the height of the economic cycle. This is mainly due to low unemployment, leading to higher incomes, so households

---

[104] https://www.telegraph.co.uk/tv/0/bbc-gold-fact-vs-fiction-extraordinary-true-story-brinks-mat/#:~:text=On%20November%2026%201983%2C%20six,six%20robbers%20were%20ever%20convicted.

tend to have more capacity to buy housing and more confidence in borrowing to purchase property. But again, when the economy slows down and perhaps goes into a recession, house prices usually fall (although not dramatically) as people cannot get a mortgage.

Furthermore, as we read earlier, the subprime mortgage crisis in America saw millions of people lose significant amounts by investing in real estate. And so you would have recognised by now that no asset is 100 per cent safe as an investment.

Therefore, where is the best place to place your investment or treasures? In the Book of Matthew, Jesus says, "Don't store up treasures here on earth where they can erode or may be stolen. Store them in Heaven where they will never lose their value and are safe from thieves."

And so, have you been investing all that you have in financial and physical assets that will no doubt be here today and gone tomorrow? If so, today might be the best time to reconsider your stock options and invest in knowing a God and Christ that can give you something that money can't buy – and that's eternal life.

Acknowledgements

I WANT TO thank the Almighty God for inspiring me to write the book and guiding me through the entire writing process. In addition, it would be amiss of me not to give a great deal of appreciation to my superwoman of a wife, Jasmyn, who has been nothing but supportive from start to finish – encouraging me every step of the way even when many chapters had to be rewritten. Indeed, you are a blessing. To my lovely daughter Layelle – whom I know most of what is written in the proceeding chapters won't make any real sense for a very long time- this is my gift to you – something I pray can be passed on to your children and your children's children. Many thanks also go to some of my favourite authors – whose books served as a gateway through which my inspiration was built. These include Aaron Ross Sorkin (Too Big to Fail), Matt Taibbi (Griftopia), Bryan Burrough and John Helyar (Barbarians At the Gate: The Fall of RJR Nabisco), Roger Lowenstein (The

End of Wall Street & When Genius Failed), Bethany McLean, Peter Elkind (The Smartest Guys in the Room).

Moreover, I would like to take this opportunity to thank the Vice Chancellor of Pentecost University, Apostle Prof. Kwabena Agyapong-Kodua, who renewed my passion for writing after I left journalism to pursue a career in education. Our work together (alongside the rest of the team – Audrey and Bella) on the weekly devotional newsletter Word Up enabled me to find a purpose behind my words. Finally, without my mother's prayers, I know I wouldn't be where I am today – so thank you, dear mum.

Printed in Great Britain
by Amazon